Get Published:

Simple Steps to Get Published and Grow Your Business with a Proven System That Works

By

Paul G. Brodie

Get Published: Simple Steps to Get Published and Grow Your Business with a Proven System That Works

Copyright @ 2018 by Paul G. Brodie

Editing by Devin Rene Mooneyham

Published in the United States by BCG Publishing, 2018.

Disclaimer

The following viewpoints in this book are those of Paul Brodie. These views are based on his personal experience over the past forty-three years on the planet Earth, especially while living in the great state of Texas.

The intention of this book is to share his story about getting published and what has worked for *him* through this journey.

All attempts have been made to verify the information provided by this publication. Neither the author nor the publisher assumes any responsibility for errors, omissions, or contrary interpretations of the subject matter herein.

This book is for entertainment purposes only. The views expressed are those of the author alone and should not be taken as expert instruction or commands. The reader is responsible for his or her future action. This book makes no guarantees of future success. However, by following the steps that are listed in this book the odds of getting published and growing your business have a much higher probability.

Neither the author nor the publisher assumes any responsibility or liability on the behalf of the purchaser or reader of these materials.

The views expressed are based on his personal experiences within the corporate world, education, and everyday life.

This book is dedicated to my mom, Barbara "Mama" Brodie. Without her support and motivation (and incredible cooking) I would literally not be here today.

I am also dedicating this book to my publishing clients, coaching clients and the student authors (past graduates, present and future students) in my Book Publishing Implementation Program. You have all gone above and beyond chasing your dreams to get published and I am proud to be able to help you accomplish your dreams.

Table of Contents

Free Webclass

Are you looking to Get Published with a proven system that works?

I want to give you access to my FREE BRAND NEW Webclass.

If you are looking to write your own book on travel, business, self-help, or anything else related to non-fiction, this Webclass is for you.

Writing a book about travel can have multiple potential tax benefits including potentially writing off most, if not all your vacation expenses.

If you are writing fiction and children's books, this online workshop is also for you.

Entrepreneurs and business owners, the benefits of writing and publishing a book is an ideal way to grow your business. Publishing a book will give you instant authority in your specific area of expertise.

This is what you will learn on this Free Online Workshop:

- **How to (Finally) Get Your Book Done, Published and in the #1 Bestseller Spot in Under 90-Days Without Having to Worry If It's "Going to Work" Or If People Are Going to Like It** (Discover the exact steps that #1 Bestselling Authors use to create a book that will drive your clients wild, create a movement and put cash in your pocket NOW)

- **How to Become a #1 Bestselling Author Even If You're Starting from Scratch and Have No Following** (Discover exactly how to use your unknown status to your advantage to get more exposure and more new clients in far less time – every single one of my clients have used this secret to become a #1 Bestselling Author)
- **How to Use Your #1 Bestselling Book to Create Multiple Streams of Income and Grow Your Business** (How anyone can use my proven "Quick and Easy Book Profits Method™ to maximize front and back-end revenue, with a steady stream of new clients that are ready to work with you - a.k.a. never chase clients again!)

FREE BONUS: Just for showing up, you'll get instant access to the Audiobook version of my #1 Bestseller, Book Publishing for Authors absolutely FREE

WARNING: The Webclass is only available for a limited time.To watch the Webclass go to www.GetPublishedSystem.com and click on the Free Webclass tab.

Foreword by Billy J. Atwell

Everyone kept telling me that I needed to publish a book in order to establish my authority as a self-confidence coach. The problem was that I had no idea how to make that possible. And whenever I asked "everyone" how to publish, they conveniently went silent.

I became frustrated, as anyone would, when continuously confronted with this Greek Chorus chanting, "You MUST publish! You MUST publish!", but without providing any guidance for this willing hero; in what was rapidly becoming a very painful tragedy.

Enter Paul Brodie.

I met Paul in the summer of 2017, when he was a guest on my podcast FEAR NOT (which has since been renamed to, *Unshakable Self-Confidence*). During our post-interview conversation, my frustration about needing to publish a book came up, to which Paul began to give me some free advice. In addition to sending me a copy of his publishing book before it launched last fall (This is one of the rewards of being a podcaster and talking to amazing people around the world, such as Paul – free gifts!).

I took his book with me on vacation, devoured it, took notes, and really began to think seriously that publishing a book could truly happen. That it wasn't some elusive dream that only happens for other people.

I reached out to Paul upon my return, discussed the best path for me (Being an athlete through-out my life, I have always worked best within the personal coach framework, so I chose to work with Paul through his One-On-One VIP Coaching Program), and proceeded to make my book a reality.

Paul laid everything out for me in a clear, time-lined series of action steps that kept me focused, accountable, and able to implement all that was necessary; including teaching me how to deal with those unforeseen roadblocks and pitfalls that come with working with editors, graphic designers, and Amazon KDP.

Because of Paul, within 60 days I went from having no manuscript, to becoming a #1 Bestselling Author. Also because of Paul, my book has remained #1 for over five months through his proven marketing system.

Whatever level you choose (whether through personal coaching, or his video modules), working with Paul will give you the best chance of becoming a published author, as Paul is amazingly generous with his knowledge; giving his all!

So, if you, dear reader, are exasperated by the endless pressure of the gods to publish, and find yourself hopeless in the dark labyrinth, read on, Paul and *Get Published* are the perfect guides to help you fulfill your quest.

Be well and peaceful.

Billy J. Atwell

Billy J. Atwell is the #1 bestselling author of Unshakable Self-Confidence. *Through his podcast and online course, he is clearing the path to peoples' self-confidence; so they can believe in themselves, achieve their goals, and enjoy their lives.*

You can find out more by visiting www.unshakableselfconfidence.com

Foreword by Sandra Joines

It's been several years since I struggled through publishing my first novel, one scrap of information at a time. Because the experience turned out to be extremely arduous and frustrating, the thought of publishing and marketing another novel tormented my soul.

After publishing became more popular, and the availability of information grew, I enrolled in an online publishing course. Finding the course difficult to apply to fiction, I switched directions and wrote a short non-fiction book, which became a #1 bestseller.

This achievement encouraged me to try again at publishing a new novel. I looked back over the course modules, thinking someone must have a simpler system. I didn't want to spend time relearning what I had forgotten; I wanted to write.

Paul Brodie is someone who I met in an online mastermind group a couple of years ago, and I have followed his successes, one bestselling book after another. After reading *Book Publishing for Authors*, I realized he had turned the complex into simple—just what I wanted. Based on his number of bestselling books, I also concluded he knew what he was doing.

Taking part in Paul Brodie's *Book Publishing Implementation Program* has been one of the best decisions I have made during my writing journey. It is the perfect combination of video modules and live group coaching calls with Paul. Not only has he developed an easy-to-follow system using his vast knowledge and experience, he has also tested his system over and over with his own books. When marketing strategies change, or when he discovers something that works better, Paul updates the program accordingly.

Paul's program takes us through the entire writing process before moving on to a clear and concise timeline that shows exactly how to navigate through the publishing and marketing journey. You can't beat this system for simplicity and results.

My best description for the *Book Publishing Implementation Program* is over-the-top incredible. It is the best program that I have taken and highly recommend it. If you are considering writing a non-fiction book, you need Paul's program.

If you are writing a fiction novel, this program is a must. It's easy to tweak to make it work well for fiction.

If you are a traditionally published author and want to give self-publishing a try, don't even think about it without checking out Paul's program.

I wanted badly for my novel to become a #1 bestseller, even though my insecurities told me it would never happen. With the step-by-step program and Paul Brodie's support and guidance, my novel became a #1 bestseller within a few days of publication.

The best investment we can make is with a proven system that works. Paul's coaching and publishing services are the real deal.

Sandra Joines

Sandra Joines is the #1 bestselling author of Shoe in the Road and Spine Surgery Recovery.

You can find out more by visiting www.SandraJoines.com

Podcast Invitation

I want to invite you to check out our brand-new podcast.

It is called Get Published and is perfect for listeners who want to get great information about the author journey in a short period of time.

Each episode is fast paced where we ask our guests 5 questions about every step of the author journey, to help you with the writing, publishing and marketing of your book.

Give us 10 minutes and we will give you a great podcast.

Get Published is hosted by Paul G. Brodie.

Go to www.GetPublishedPodcast.com to check out the Get Published Podcast.

Introduction

Welcome to my third publishing book. This is not your typical how to publishing book. It is for people who want to know how to write a book quickly and in the most efficient manner possible. This book is for people who want to get published with a proven system that works. If you want to use your book to grow your business then this book is for you. Having your own book is the modern-day business card and is the way to be able to sell your services to the warmest leads possible.

Many of the costs involved with getting your book published are tax deductible. Always check with your accountant first, but the investment of hiring a book publishing coach or a book publisher, in order to get published, are often tax deductible. Travel costs are also often tax deductible, as I have written multiple travel books due to my love of travel and for the tax benefits. We will cover much more about this within the book.

Have you always wanted to write a book? Do you find it difficult to know where to start? Has a family member or friend said that you should write a book?

I want to tell you that everyone has a book in them and this book will help you get published with a proven system that works. One of the biggest challenges about writing your own book is getting started. We all struggle with sharing ourselves with the world and writing your own book can appear scary. I can assure you that if I can write 12 bestselling books, then you can as well. This is what we will cover in get published:

Chapter 1: Everyone has a book in them

Chapter 2: How to run your book like a business

Chapter 3: Choosing your title and subtitle and why both are critical in the success of your book

Chapter 4: Designing your book cover with the end in mind

Chapter 5: Creating your outline with both the content and the structure of your offers in the book

Chapter 6: Creating your book and whether to write, speak and record your book - how to expand on each section of your outline

Chapter 7: Why you should invest in having a great editor

Chapter 8: Formatting your book

Chapter 9: Create a book description that sells

Chapter 10: Creating an author biography and what to include

Chapter 11: Building your website

Chapter 12: Getting reviews as soon as your book is published

Chapter 13: Marketing your book launch

I hope that this book helps you in your journey to get published. My philosophy in anything I do in life, whether it's teaching, giving motivational seminars, and writing and coaching, is to have the power of one. The power of one is my goal to help at least one person. I hope that person is you.

Free Book

I would like to offer you the digital version of Book Publishing for Beginners. The brand-new second edition of Book Publishing for Beginners will only be available on the website for a limited time. Enjoy!

Go to www.BrodieEDU.com/bp to grab your free copy of Book Publishing for Beginners.

Chapter 1 Everyone Has a Book in Them

"You have something special inside you. Something you know. Something you do. Something you can teach. You are already an expert." Robert Kiyosaki

Have you always wanted to write a book? Do you find it difficult to know where to start?

Would you like someone to introduce you as a bestselling author? Could you imagine if that happened to you? Are you ready to get started in your author journey?

I started this chapter with multiple questions because I want to tell you that everyone has a book in them. This book will help you get published with a proven system that works. One of the biggest challenges about writing your own book is getting started.

Author is the root word for authority. It gives you instant credibility and positions you as an expert in your area of expertise.

That is why writing a book is critical to every business owner who wants to grow his or her business. I help my clients in the United States, United Kingdom, Canada, Australia, and New

Zealand to get published with our proven system that works.

This year I joined both the Arlington Chamber of Commerce and the Arlington Sunrise Rotary Club so I could give back and connect with local businesses. Service to others is something that I live by, as my personal motto is Veritas et Utilitas, which translates roughly to truth and service. Those are also the two core values of my company.

With truth, I view truth as being completely honest and direct with my clients. This also includes complete transparency as I walk them through the entire writing and publishing process including timelines.

When I was introduced to both the chamber and Rotary, I was introduced as an 11-time bestselling author. It immediately got the attention of those in the room and I had multiple people approach me to ask about my business, as well as how I could help them write a book. As I mentioned earlier, the root word of authority is author and gives you both instant credibility and a warm introduction to people you want to meet.

My response to every person who approached me was that everyone has a book in them and you don't even need to write your book. That's right! I told perspective clients they don't even have to write their own book. Instead, they could speak out their book by using several different software programs. I will go more into detail about the programs later in this book, as creating your own book is excuse proof. They could start in moments by downloading an app from the app store either for their iPhone or for Android and speak out their book.

On the app that I recommend, there is a button you can press that will send the audio recording to the company. They charge one dollar per minute of recorded audio and they will transcribe the book into text and send you the transcription within 12 hours. I will talk more about how you can do this in chapter 6 and how you can repurpose content from your website, blogs, PowerPoint slide shows, research, and trainings into your book.

This opened the eyes of my prospective new clients and within three days, I landed my first client from the Arlington Chamber of Commerce. His name is Scott and he is speaking out his entire book. Once his book is completed, my company will be both publishing and marketing his book through our Done For You Publishing and Book Launch Marketing Services.

All he will do once his book is completed, is send me his final draft and my company will take care of the rest. This includes getting his book edited, creating a custom book cover design, formatting the book to Kindle and Paperback, creating a custom book description and uploading the book. This service also includes a strategy session that will help him get crystal clear vision with the book and what he wants to get out of it.

What I just covered is my Done For You Book Publishing Service and how I help my clients get published once they have completed their draft. After we receive the draft, we then spend the next 30 days getting the book ready.

We will get the book edited during the first 14 days. During that period, we will also create a custom book cover. The book cover is created through collaboration with our clients, as we want everything to be done correctly and to the satisfaction of the client. Once the edits and book cover are completed and approved by the client, we will then start the formatting process, which takes up the following 14 days. The book is formatted into both Kindle and Paperback. We then create the book description, all during this period.

The process typically takes a month, as we want everything to be done correctly and with the highest quality in mind. We take great pride in our quality because you do get what you pay for in life. Once the book is formatted, then we will upload the book online and if needed will create the custom marketing plan for those clients who want me to launch their book through our Done For You Book Launch Marketing Service. It is same marketing system that has launched all my books to a #1 bestseller and all my client's books. This is a proven system that works and is used for non-fiction, fiction, and children's books. It fully aligns with our core values, as we walk our clients through the entire process so everything is crystal clear. We want to take the mystery out of the publishing process by being truthful, transparent, and giving the best customer service possible as we care not only about the client, but also the person.

Our Done For You Book Launch Marketing Service also offers a bestseller guarantee, which means this is not only a service, it is a promise. Through this service, you will become a #1 bestselling author and have instant credibility to help grow your business. We also show you how to increase your book's exposure by 400 percent by getting your book into an additional eight categories on Amazon. One of the questions I receive the most from my clients is, how does a book become a #1 bestseller?

You will hear many answers on that question and I want to be completely transparent as being truthful is the foundation on which my company is built on. We define a #1 bestselling author as someone whose book reaches #1 in at least one category on Amazon. This is not a gimmick where you are #1 for an hour or two. My service guarantees that you will be #1 in your category for at least one week. This is like when a new movie or music album comes out; they are categorized by ranking #1 for one week to be consider a hit.

Billy Atwell is a client of mine who I helped get published and built him a custom marketing game-plan. He wanted to grow both his coaching service and the audience for his podcast. While working with Billy, we created an amazing book cover, custom book description and implemented a marketing plan where he had great success with his launch. His book, Unshakable Self-Confidence was launched in early January 2018 and is still #1 in at least one category many months later. Our system works.

I bring this up because I do not want to waste your time. This book is all about having a proven system that works. If you are going to write a book, then you will be able to maximize the exposure of becoming a #1 bestselling author while increasing your revenue on both the front-end and back-end with our proven system.

One of the biggest changes for my company is our addition of Done For You Publishing and Marketing Services over the past year. This was done based on the demand to fill the needs of those who want to get published, but do not have the time to learn how to do it themselves. People are busy, especially business owners and time is limited.

I have many people in my Book Publishing Implementation Program who want to learn how to get their book published. However, many business owners do not want to learn about how to publish and market their book due to time constraints. Instead, they give me their draft and we take care of everything from that point on.

The reason I bring up my services is because I feel that getting published is potentially life-changing to both you and your business. Getting published correctly and with a proven system that works is key to the success of your book. I learned from the great Russell Brunson (Founder of Click Funnels) in his Expert Secrets book that we have a moral obligation to share our message because it is life changing and can help others. I have seen how my client's lives have changed with getting published and I want to help you do the same.

The main thing to know about writing a book is that everyone has a book in them and that you must run your book like a business. In the next chapter, that is exactly what I am going to show you.

To find out more about our services go to www.GetPublishedSystem.com and click on the services tab.

Chapter 2 Running Your Book like a Business

"To each there comes in their lifetime a special moment when they are figuratively tapped on the shoulder and offered the chance to do a very special thing, unique to them and fitted to their talents. What a tragedy if that moment finds them unprepared or unqualified for that which could have been their finest hour." Sir. Winston Churchill

Would you like to use your book to grow your business? Now that you have decided to get published you need to answer one critical question before you start writing. What do you want to get out of your book?

Do you want to grow your business with your book? Is creating the book something that you want to check off your bucket list? Do you want to write a children's book for your child? Do you want to become a fiction author? Do you want to sell a new service with the book? What services do you want to offer?

We all have one shot to make a first impression with our readers. With that shot, you must realize that your book is the key to growing your business and you must run it like a business and not a hobby.

Running your book like a business is critical to your future success and you must know what you want to get out of your book before getting started. Another question to answer is, how will your book help other people?

Is your book going to teach someone how to do something? My first book Eat Less and Move More covered my struggle with weight. I taught others how to live a healthier lifestyle and showed them how they could lose weight and most importantly keep the weight off. This was something deeply personal to me because in 2011, I was close to 340 pounds, had multiple health issues to a point where my Doctor said I would be dead in five years if I didn't get my act together.

Over the next year, I lost 60 pounds and kept the weight off. What was the secret? I chose to eat less and move more and wanted to share both the victories and setbacks with losing weight.

My second book was about building my speaking business. It is called Motivation 101. I wrote it over a one-week period after I finished Eat Less and Move More. Motivation 101 became my second bestseller and I increased my speaking fee from $500.00 to $3000.00 per speech due to the success of the book.

This was accomplished through my motivational seminar called Motivation 101. I took the content of the seminar as the basis for the outline and book. Once I started writing, I expanded on each point in the book. The biggest difference maker was when I gave the seminar at conferences and then mentioned that I was a #1 bestselling author and that I wrote a book based on the seminar.

It gave me instant credibility and authority and getting bookings was easier than ever. If you want to get published to increase your speaking business, then I can tell you that having your own book is the quickest way to increase your speaking fee. You will be able to use the book to leverage your authority as a #1 bestselling author and grow your business.

Selling services is another thing to look at. Initially, I wrote my books to help people who were struggling with weight and to increase business for my speaking business. Then a funny thing happened that was completely unexpected…

Readers and fellow authors began contacting me and asked if I could help them get published. At the time, I published my third bestseller called Positivity Attracts. The book was launched around

Thanksgiving 2015 and was my biggest success yet. Positivity Attracts combined with my two other books brought me the first of many four figure months in royalties. It also got the attention of many people who also wanted to become a #1 bestselling author.

People often ask me if I went through a publishing course or had personal coaching when I started out. I always made clear that I was self-taught. Everything I learned was the hard way and through many hours of research, trial and error, listening to author summits, podcasts, reading articles, and learning as much as possible about marketing.

Additionally, it is why I am a huge believer in either hiring a coach or utilizing a book publisher to help you as it will accelerate your journey to get published. Hiring a coach or a book publisher will help you get published much faster than doing it yourself because it will help you with focus, accountability, speed, and support. This is why I offer Done For You services with my company, in addition to coaching. I want to help my clients get published quickly with systems that are proven to work.

What I did learn after launching three straight bestsellers, was that I had developed both a book publishing and book marketing system and that I could help many people with their books. This is when I decided to write my fourth book over the Christmas holiday in 2015.

At the time, I was still teaching and made time to write between Christmas and New Year's. I wrote Book Publishing for Beginners during that time and launched the book in January. This was a different experience, as I not only made revenue on the front-end with royalties for Kindle, Paperback, and Audiobook, but also with the back-end as I started to take on clients. I helped coach others one-on-one with how to get published. It was just like teaching and I realized that I could make a living helping others with their books.

In 2017, I left teaching to focus on my publishing business. I hired an amazing coach in early 2017 who helped me scale my business quickly and showed me how to create a group-coaching program. That program became the Book Publishing Implementation Program and I could help coach people through both the program and through our One-On-One VIP Coaching Program for those who needed additional support.

As you have noticed with my story, having my own book was life changing. I am now able to help my clients get published and more importantly help them in their author journey. Do you see how this can change your business?

Go to www.BrodieEDU.com/gps to download my free checklist on different ways to run your book like a business.

Chapter 3 Choosing Your Title and Subtitle

Choosing your title and subtitle is critical to the success of your book. Have you decided on the name for your book title? Do you feel that the book title stands out? When it comes to choosing a book title, you want to choose one that will be easy to search for on Amazon.

Amazon is essentially a giant search engine. When you type in certain phrases, you will notice this trend. I suggest trying this yourself. Once you are on Amazon, go to the search engine on Amazon, click the search tab on the left side of the search bar, change search tab from "all departments" to "kindle store".

If you already have chosen your book title, then type in the first word of the book title and see what comes up in the search results. Your book title does need to connect with the content in your book.

Some great book title examples are: The 4 Hour Workweek, Awaken The Giant Within, How to Win Friends and Influence People, To Kill a Mockingbird, Rich Dad Poor Dad, The 7 Habits of Highly Effective People.

What makes those book titles great? The titles are eye-catching and get your attention. The titles are also easy to understand. When I decided on Eat Less and Move More for my first book, I wanted the title to connect with fitness, my own journey, and the point of the book, the outcome.

I was a teacher for nine years and one of the greatest lessons I have learned is that we must make things as simple as possible. Don't make an overly complex or complicated title. You also want to have a strong subtitle.

Have you chosen a subtitle for your book? Does the subtitle that you have chosen stand out? The subtitle of your book is the benefit to the reader. For example, most of my books focus on ten ways to help the reader. In Motivation 101, the subtitle is ten ways to increase your motivation. The subtitle is clear with the benefit to the reader. Remember, the subtitle should always include the benefit to your reader.

When I created my third book, I already decided on the title as it was based on one of my motivational seminars. The book was called Positivity Attracts. If you type the word positivity in Amazon, the results are quite impressive. Anything with the word positive or a variation of the word (like positivity) gets many search results on Amazon.

The subtitle of Positivity Attracts showed the benefit with ten ways to improve your positive thinking. My subtitles are typically short and to the point. Simplicity is always best with choosing both your title and subtitle.

My travel books also followed this formula. The main thing about my travel books is that the title is always the location. Both my Maui books are titled Maui, but with different subtitles. The first book about Maui was published in 2016 and has the subtitle of ten ways to enjoy the best food, beaches, and locations while on vacation. My second book about Maui was published in 2018 and has a lot of updated information from the 2017 trip including lots of new content. The 2018 Maui book has the subtitle of ten ways to get the most out of your vacation.

I also wrote a travel book in 2017 about San Diego. I used San Diego as the title and used the same subtitle as the 2016 Maui book. The travel books are all #1 bestsellers and I highly recommend using the title of the city if you plan on writing a travel book.

My two previous publishing books focused more on the how to process with completing your book. The first book was called Book Publishing for Beginners and the second book was called Book Publishing for Authors. The focus on both books was to show specific results in the subtitle.

In Book Publishing for Beginners, the subtitle and benefit is how to publish and market your book to a #1 bestseller and grow your business. Book Publishing for Authors was published last fall and the subtitle was more time sensitive. The subtitle was how to write, publish and market your book to a #1 bestseller in the next 90 days. Book Publishing for Beginners covered more about what to do once your first draft is completed while Book Publishing for Authors showed you how to write your book, publish your book, and market your book.

Get Published is different compared to those two other publishing books because we are focusing more on the why versus the how. I am specifically writing this book for people who want to use a book to not only grow a business, but also want to finish their draft through either writing the book, speaking it out and having it transcribed, and repurposing content from your website, blogs,

PowerPoint slide shows, research, and trainings into your book.

This book is also less technical and I wanted that conveyed in the subtitle. It is why we specifically stated that the benefit of this book is simple steps to get published and grow your business with a proven system that works. All three areas of the subtitle address simplifying, getting published, and doing it with a proven system that works.

The steps covered in this book go through successful launches and why they worked. It is a proven system and all you must do is trust the process. When it comes to your book title, have a title that will grab the attention of the reader. Remember that the subtitle is the benefit that people will get out of reading your book. Now that you have thought about the title and subtitle, it is now time to start thinking about what you want your book cover to look like. Are you ready to finalize your book title?

Go to www.BrodieEDU.com/gps to download a list of great book titles to help with your book.

Chapter 4 Designing Your Book Cover

The book cover is your packaging. You need to have great packaging as your book cover is as important as the content in your book. This is the main reason why I have always utilized book cover designers.

Have you thought about what you want your book cover to look like? In my previous publishing books, I always waited until after the book was written, before bringing up the cover. In Get Published, I want you to start thinking about your book cover before your book is completed. I had book covers made for every one of my books before the draft was completed, except for my first book.

Having the book cover created before the draft was completed helped for several reasons. The first was inspiration. Even though you may not have your book cover completed, I know that you have an idea for where you want to go. When I am helping my clients with their covers, I always tell them to visualize the cover and what they want to see. From that point, I help them make that vision a reality.

Consider the following questions. What color do you want in the background of the book cover? What color do you want the book title text to be in? Should the subtitle text have the same color as the main title? What image should you use for the book cover?

Having a great looking book cover is one of the most important parts about having a successful book launch. Readers do judge a book by its cover and you will want to have the best-looking book cover possible.

When you are deciding on your book cover, you want to look at several factors. You want the cover to be eye-catching. It needs to grab the attention of the reader.

You also want to have great colors in the cover. Orange has proven to sell well as that color not only stands out, but also elicits a buying response in potential customers. Having a bold font in the book title is also important, as you want to have the actual title stand out.

As I mentioned previously, the subtitle is also crucial and tells readers the benefits of your book. Make sure that your subtitle stands out visually with a great looking font and color. You want to have a very clear subtitle and tell the reader why your book will help them solve a problem.

The cover needs to look great in the thumbnail view on Amazon. When you do a search of books on Amazon, you will see the results in list form. The book covers will be in a much smaller format, otherwise known as a thumbnail view. Having a great looking cover with a clear and bold title will stand out, especially when competing with other books for the reader's attention.

The thumbnail view also comes into play on book sales rankings. When you click on a book you will see the sales ranking of the book and will be able to click on that ranking and see other books in that category. Your book cover is shown in the thumbnail form and will stand out if it looks good.

The book cover is your window dressing. Choosing the right book cover is critical to your book becoming a #1 bestseller, or just another book. Covers can range in cost from five dollars to several thousand dollars. As I had a small budget for my first book, Eat Less and Move More, I knew that I needed to get as much bang for the buck as possible.

This was in 2015 and I researched Fiverr extensively and found a freelancer who made book covers for a very inexpensive cost and had a great rating from customers. In fact, she has thousands of ratings so I figured I would give it a shot. I was not disappointed.

Everything on Fiverr is at least five dollars to start, but there are always extras. I chose the twenty-dollar option for my first three books, which included the five-dollar gig, an additional five dollars for a high-quality stock image, and ten dollars for the original PSD file and PDF. This was a great investment so I could have the master copy in case I ever needed to make any changes.

In my request for my first book cover, I asked for a blue and black color scheme. Within four days, my designer delivered my first book cover and I loved it.

Vikiana has made the book covers for my books between 2015 and through summer of 2017. She has done good work for the price. This was the book cover design that Vikiana created for my first book.

It was a good cover to start my publishing career. As you can see, my subtitle was not strong. In 2019, I am planning on writing and publishing the sequel for Eat Less and Move More and have a subtitle with a definable outcome like my other books. In the sequel, I have the subtitle as Ten Ways to Help You Lose Weight and Keep the Weight Off. With that book, I have a clear subtitle with a definable outcome.

If I ever go back and change the first book, I will add more of a definable outcome. I was still proud of the title and subtitle overall and how the book started to build the momentum in my own author journey as my first bestselling book.

I had a different problem with Motivation 101, my second book. Problem was that I hated the book cover. When you do not like your book cover then you must trust your gut, and make changes. Here is the original cover:

The cover did not fit and clearly was not worth even a few dollars for the design. Seeing the ugly brown shoes, in addition to the poor placement of the subtitle, made me realize that my second book would not be successful if I launched the book with that cover. I decided that I needed to make a change.

I reached out to Vikiana and created a new order. In the order, I told her that I wanted a new cover and my vision for the cover was of a sunset with Motivation 101 still in bold on top of the cover. I also made clear that I wanted the subtitle just below the main title. This is what she created for me for five dollars (six dollars with service fee) as I did not order any extras since it was a new design.

The cover was a significant upgrade and I felt great about the book cover. I ordered additional covers for the audiobook version and the paperback version. Typically, you can order the audiobook cover version for ten dollars and the paperback version will cost you twenty-five dollars. I knew that the new cover would help make my second book a bestseller and it did.

I do want to stress that you will get what you pay for. In September 2017, I decided to part ways with Vikiana and hired a new cover designer exclusively for my book covers. His work is excellent and I have used him for Book Publishing for Authors, Champion, Maui (my second Maui book), Las Vegas, and Get Published. While he is a lot more expensive, you get what you pay for. He was highly recommended by a fellow author and has done a great job on the book covers that he has created for my company. I now utilize him exclusively for my client's book covers.

Here are examples of the book covers he has made for my books. As you can see, it took my book covers to the next level. Therefore, I added him to my publishing team due to the high quality of his work.

He also created a new cover for Book Publishing for Beginners for the second edition that was released in early 2018. Below is the original white cover from when it was initially published in 2016, and the new red cover that he created.

Having a great looking cover that grabs the attention of the reader is critical. Before we wrap up this chapter, I want to share how you can create a rough mockup of your own cover. I am a terrible artist and cannot draw at all. However, I can do some basic design concepts. If I can create a rough mockup of a cover, then anyone can.

When I think of a book cover design, I do searches on google. I find images that I feel will fit the cover and then figure out the placement of where I want the title, subtitle, background cover, and image design. You always want your title on the top part of your book.

When creating a book cover you want to be able to see the book cover in both a regular and thumbnail view. Once you have a general idea of what you want then you can send the information to your book cover designer and make clear what you want in the cover design.

One thing I will do is create a mock design in Microsoft Word. I will create the book title with the font and color that I want. Below the font and color will be the design image that I want in the cover. Once everything is done, I will send it to my cover designer.

By using that process, you should be able to come up with a great book cover design. I also recommend downloading book covers that you like on Amazon that you feel stand out. Create a folder on your computer with the title, book covers, and save every book cover that you like in that file. You will have a great library of book covers to help you find inspiration for your book cover design.

If you are looking for some great cover designs, then check out my own book page on www.GetPublishedSystem.com to get some ideas. I also recommend looking up the following book covers: The 4 Hour Workweek, The Devil Wears Prada, To Kill A Mockingbird, Rich Dad Poor Dad, The 7 Habits Of Highly Effective People. Are you ready to start creating your book cover?

Go to www.BrodieEDU.com/gps to download over fifty examples of great looking book covers.

Chapter 5 Creating Your Outline

"A good plan violently executed now is better than a perfect plan executed next week." George S. Patton

Before you start to write your book, you need to create an outline. Outlining the book will help you execute the plan for the content of your book. My first experience outlining a book was at the pool at The Mirage Hotel and Casino in Las Vegas. During that morning, I spent around an hour coming up with the outline while enjoying the morning summer heat in Sin City.

Typing that outline into my iPhone created a structure and direction for my first book. I have used the same process for each of my books and my clients are strongly encouraged to start their book by creating an outline.

When creating your first draft, do not worry about it being perfect. The main thing is to create a game plan through writing out your outline. Writing out the outline will help get you clear on what you want to write in your book. It will also help with the pace and timeline of your writing content.

Start with figuring out the front matter of your book. The front matter will include an offer, forward, introduction, and possibly a second offer.

In this book, the front matter is the free Webclass (highly recommend investing an hour to watch it), two forewords (social proof from someone who has worked with you), invitation to check out my new podcast, introduction (preview your book and tell the reader what to expect), a second offer (in this book I offer the free digital download of Book Publishing for Beginners), and then start thinking about your chapters, otherwise known as your talking points.

Think about at least ten talking points for your book, once you have those talking points, you then have chapters. Each talking point is a chapter in your book. Once you have your talking points/chapters, then start at chapter one and expand on that first point. Then do the same for the rest of your talking points/chapters. We will cover this more in depth in our next chapter on how to write your book.

After uncovering at least ten talking points/chapters, it is time to add your back matter. The back matter includes a call to action, a list of other books that you have (great for when you have multiple books published), about the author, acknowledgements, contact information, and feedback request.

In my books, I have the following in the back matter: strategy session invitation (to set up a quick call with me so I can help you get published), more books by Paul (where you can access my other books), acknowledgements (to thank those who have supported you), contact information (include website, Facebook, Twitter, Instagram, LinkedIn, and any other social media accounts where your readers can find you), feedback request (ask readers to leave a review and to contact you on ways to improve the book).

Another nice benefit is once you outline your book you will see potential opportunities to expand your book into a book series. When I wrote Motivation 101, Chapter 4 of the book was called Just Do It. I found a lot of great content with that chapter where I could create another book that was released during Thanksgiving 2016.

Just Do It began as a chapter in Motivation 101, then became a seminar and then eventually evolved into my seventh bestselling book. When I originally created my first seminar in 2007, it was called PMA: Positive Mental Attitude. It was a motivational seminar that later became my eighth bestselling book. Through that seminar, I always created new content.

The additional content from PMA became Positivity Attracts. Once I had enough new content for Positivity Attracts, the next seminar created was Motivation 101. When I had enough content for Motivation 101, I created the seminar for The Pursuit of Happiness. After I had enough content for The Pursuit of Happiness, the next seminar became Just Do It. When I had everything completed and updated for Just Do It, I created Champion.

I share this process because of the power of outlining your content. All my original seminars had outlines and it was easy to translate the outlines into the books. You can do the same thing with your content, otherwise known as IP. Your IP is your Intellectual Property. The IP is your content that you create for your books, seminars, coaching, courses, website, blogs, PowerPoint slide shows, and trainings. It is the knowledge that you have which you turned into your content.

Outlining is a great way to be clear on what you are going to write. The best part is that you will most likely be able to find more content then you need for your book. You can utilize the additional content to create additional books as part of a book series.

Having an outline provides you with clarity as you write your book. The outline will also help ensure that your book flows and connects with the title, subtitle, and content throughout your book. Are you ready to start outlining your book?

Go to www.Facebook.com and type "Get Published" in the search bar to join me, current, and aspiring authors in my Get Published Facebook Community to get additional support with your book outline.

Chapter 6 Writing Your Book

"The journey of a thousand miles begins with one step." Lao Tzu

Now that you have your book title, subtitle, and outline, it is time to start writing your book. Does the thought of writing your book sound scary? Do you worry about how you can write your book? I want to assure you that it is not difficult and you can accomplish it in a variety of ways. Remember, the main thing is to get started by taking the first step.

The first option is to write your book. I am old school and enjoy writing. Writing has always been a great love of mine, so for me, I know my best method is to write my book via Microsoft Word. It is how I am writing this chapter on the couch of my living room where I have created many of my books. I can look outside the window at my patio and pool, and is a great source of inspiration.

When traveling, one of my favorite places to write is on the lanai of the condo where I stay when I'm in Maui. I wrote three books from that lanai in Kihei while watching amazing views of the west side of Maui and the Pacific Ocean. Find a place where you are comfortable and productive. You always need inspiration when creating your book.

There is another method that I have mentioned already in this book, and that is to speak out your book. Download the Rev app on your smart phone and use it to record your book. You can also use software like Dragon Speak if you prefer. I like Rev because it is easy to use and can be used on your phone and can record the audio wherever and whenever you want to.

Speaking out your book makes the process excuse proof. You can speak out your book in the car, during lunch, at home; you could even speak it in the bathroom. We all literally have our phones tethered to our side and you have opportunities throughout the day to get your book done. Creating your book through this method is excuse proof.

I suggest that you focus on one chapter at a time and start speaking specifically about that chapter. When you are done talking, you will have a recording of your session. There is a transcribe button on the bottom of the app. All you need to do is press that button for more information. As an example, I took part in a talk to my leads group at the Arlington Chamber of Commerce with several of my strategic business partners. I pressed the record button and it recorded our brief talk. The total time of the talk was 10 minutes and 10 seconds.

At the end of the talk, I announced to the group that we recorded the session and could use that information to write a chapter in the book. All I needed to do was to press the transcribe button at the bottom of the app and then follow the instructions. I would have the recording transcribed with 99 percent accuracy and a money back guarantee from Rev if I was not completely satisfied with the transcription.

Ten minutes of audio is perfect for a chapter of a book, especially non-fiction. I hit the transcribe button and found that it would cost me only a dollar per minute to have the audio transcribed and I would receive the file within 12 hours of sending it. You also receive a special ten dollars off discount for your first order. I announced to the group that we had just recorded our talk on Rev, which at over 10 minutes, was the basis for a full chapter of a book. It got the attention of the business owners in the room and several downloaded Rev that day to help with their book.

Speaking out your book is excuse proof. In other words, there is no excuse as to why you cannot get your book completed within the next 90 days, if not sooner. I do have clients that take longer and that is fine. However, you can get your book completed quickly whether you speak it out or write the book.

I wrote my third book, Positivity Attracts in less than 24 hours. The outline was already complete, as it was based on one of my motivational seminars. I could expand on each of the ten talking points and was ready to send it to my editor one day later.

You can also repurpose content if it is yours. Blogs are a great example. My friend, Corey, has written over 8000 words from blogs on his website. Corey mentioned that two of my strategic business partners were helping him with his website and told him that he has enough content to write a book. My strategic partners knew from me that you need a minimum of 8000 words to write a book. Corey is planning to take that content to create his first book about financial planning with the content from his website.

As I mentioned in the last chapter, all my original seminars had outlines and it was easy to translate the outlines to the books. You can do the same thing with your content, otherwise known as IP. Your IP is your Intellectual Property. The IP is your content that you create for your books, seminars, online coaching, blogs, courses etc. It is the knowledge that you have which you turned into your content.

When creating your book, you can write or speak it in the order of your outline or you can create it out of the outline order. Typically, I recommend creating your book in the order of your outline. However, if there is a chapter that you absolutely must write first, then I encourage you to do so.

One of the main questions that I get from my clients is, how much time should I set aside each day to create my book? Everyone is different with his or her creative process. There is not a universal process for everyone.

What I typically like to find out is my client's process. Are they the type of person who highly organizes their day? If that is the case, I recommend they block out one – two hours a day to create their book. The potential goal could be to complete a chapter a day.

If my clients are more like me and prone to writing/speaking when the inspiration hits, then I recommend starting to write/speak as much as you can in one sitting. I always recommend taking breaks every ninety minutes to get a drink, refresh, and get up and stretch.

Everyone is going to be different and you need to find the style that fits you best. For my own books, I have written several of them over three to four days. When I wrote Positivity Attracts, I literally could not stop writing and in one day had written over ten thousand words for the book. Again, it depends on your own personal style.

Using either method will ensure that you have your book completed within two - three weeks. I recommend that you have someone who will keep you accountable with your book writing. Whether that is investing in a book publishing coach like myself, or relying on a good friend or family member, having accountability, focus, and encouragement throughout the writing process is critical.

If you have my style of writing/speaking and do so when the inspiration hits, then give yourself a goal to finish your book in three weeks. That way you have a deadline and know that even though you are not specifically setting time daily to create your book, you do need to have your book done in three weeks. You could also set the goal to complete four chapters in a week to get started. Again, you must figure out what is the best route for you. Deadlines will make all the difference in getting your book completed.

The main thing is that everyone has at least one book in them. Whether you write or speak out your book, the point is to share your story. You want to connect to the reader. The reader wants to connect to you through your story. Do not be afraid to be vulnerable, as it will build a strong connection with the reader.

The Pursuit of Happiness was the hardest book that I wrote. Not due to any challenges with word count, but with the subject matter. I wrote about my childhood and when I severely bullied in the sixth grade. Originally, I was not sure if I wanted to write that chapter in the book as it would leave me very vulnerable and covering that subject made me think of those days once again. I also wrote about fighting depression, family issues, and even being what would be defined as homeless for several months in my teenage years. The best thing I did was letting go and writing that entire book. It built strong connections between the reader and me and was therapeutic as a writer to share my story. Two years later, the book still sells well, has many great reviews, and was listed as a bestseller as recently as May 2018.

Regardless of which method you use, realize that your book doesn't have to be perfect. Once the book is done, do not second-guess yourself. You have already taken the plunge and now it is time to send the first draft to your editor.

Before we move on, I want to share the feedback that I received from one of my students who graduated from my Book Publishing Implementation program. This is the group-coaching program that I encourage aspiring authors to utilize if they have the time to do so and want to learn about the writing, publishing, and marketing process.

Most business owners do not have the time to learn how to do it themselves and instead want me to publish it for them. However, if you are a do it yourself type of person and need some additional support then check out what Elizabeth shared about working with me and my team. I am sharing her feedback in this chapter, as Elizabeth's goal has been to write a book for the past forty years.

"Joining Paul Brodie's 'Book Publishing Implementation Program' has re-ignited my passion for writing. Mr. Brodie's coaching expertise, encouragement, inspiration and transparency has motivated me to pursue my forty-year dream of composing non-fiction books. Through his extremely user friendly and in-depth weekly Training Modules, he leaves no stone unturned as he shares his personal experiences about manuscripts, book covers and titles, editors, publishers, etc. Mr. Brodie also provides invaluable real-time online Live Group Coaching. During these sessions, he not only answers my questions on the spot, he communicates through email after the Webinar is over. I highly recommend Mr. Brodie's program to anyone seeking the same dream I have of becoming a published author. I am going on sixty years of age and experiencing the reality of it is never too late to put that pen to paper and let your words flow. Cheers to you, Paul Brodie!" Elizabeth Vidad

We do offer help on the writing portion of your book through our Book Publishing Implementation Program. If you prefer one-on-one support, you can get that through our One-

On-One VIP Coaching program where I will personally help you get your book written. At this point, we have completed the writing process and will next move to the publishing part of the book. I do want you to think about this, what has been the most useful so far?

Please write down what has been the most useful to you so far before you move on to the publishing part of the book.

Chapter 7 Invest in a Great Editor

I want to tell you one of the biggest secrets about getting published. The difficult, time-consuming part is not the writing/speaking part. That is the easiest part. The most difficult part is the editing process.

Having a great editor will transform your book and is critical to your book's success. An editor will typically catch eighty to ninety percent of your mistakes and will not only find the mistakes, but also will make suggestions or corrections.

You must invest in having a great editor as having your draft edited correctly is just as important as having a great looking book cover. A poorly edited book with multiple spelling mistakes will cost you both short-term and long-term sales through refunds from unhappy readers. You could get negative reviews due to multiple spelling, grammar, and punctuation mistakes. An editor will find most, if not all your errors. They will also clean up grammar and spelling mistakes and will clean up your draft into a manuscript that is ready to get published. Remember that a poorly edited book will hurt not only your book, but also your brand and business.

An editor could be a friend or family member or you can find a freelancer on Fiverr or Upwork. You can also ask other authors whom they would recommend. The most important thing is to find a quality editor for your book as you only get one chance to make a first impression with your readers.

In July 2015, I wrote my first book Eat Less and Move More over three days. After my first draft was ready to go, I reached out to a friend of mine who is an excellent book editor. Her name is Devin Mooneyham (Mooneyham.Devin@gmail.com) and she has served as the editor for all my books. Devin sliced and diced my first draft editing the grammatical errors, sentence fragments, and took out parts of chapters that did not flow.

I trusted Devin completely with this huge part of the process and ever since our partnership has been wonderful. Having a great editor is critical and something I consider the most crucial part of finishing your book.

You can find very good editors on Fiverr.com or on Upwork.com. Editing can range anywhere from several hundred dollars to over one thousand dollars, so finding the right editor is very important. The fee will also vary depending on how many words are in your book. If your book is over twenty-five thousand words, then you can expect to pay more for an editor as the editing process can be very time consuming.

As my company has expanded to add the Done For You publishing services, I hired a second editor to join the team. Devin is still my personal editor and does help several of my coaching clients. Due to time commitments, she only edits on a part-time basis. I needed to bring on a second editor exclusively for my Done For You publishing clients. The editor I brought on edits full-time and has helped fellow author friends of mine in the past with many of their books, like the outstanding editing that Devin has done for me.

With our Done For You services all you do is send me your first draft and everything else is taken care of for you. We take care of the hard part with getting your book edited. All the editing is done within 14 days and you will receive the edited final draft. At that point, we will only proceed once you have given us the approval to format your book. While our service is Done For You, we want to be as collaborative as possible to ensure complete satisfaction by our clients.

Our company's core values with truth and service connect with our services and there are many great publishers who will publish your book correctly. Many of them charge between 15 to 30 thousand dollars for Done For You publishing services. However, there are publishers who do not take care of their clients and I have had many clients who have come to me after being screwed by another publisher.

It is always heartbreaking to hear their stories about how publishers have promised them the moon and have essentially conned them out of significant money ranging from five thousand dollars to over ten thousand dollars. This happens a lot more than you think as there are many people out there who want to make a quick sale and steal money from good people who have a life-long dream of getting their book published.

I have heard of publishers who have disappeared completely after taking their money and essentially robbed good people of their life savings. Some have even skipped down with tens of thousands of dollars from people they have scammed. Fortunately, I have been able to help those clients get published and put them on the path to become bestselling authors through either our Book Publishing Implementation Program, One-On-One VIP Coaching, or through our Done For You Book Publishing and Book Launch Marketing Services.

Transparency is key when you are working with a publisher. We are completely transparent with the process and timeline. It is a one-month process to get your book published from when you send me your book. After a strategy session with my clients, I will go through the timeline and walk them through the entire process through our Done For You Publishing Service.

The first 14 days involve the editing of your book and we design your book cover. Once both the final draft is ready and the book cover is done, we send both to you for approval. If changes need to be made, then we will make changes. After you approve both the final edited draft and book cover, we will get your book formatted while creating your book description.

The book description is sent to you for approval and once approved, we will get your book uploaded to Amazon for Kindle, CreateSpace for paperback, and as a bonus will show you how you can have the audiobook version created for free. This is done through a narrator on Audible with their royalty share agreement and you will make a profit with the first audiobook sale. We will also create you a hardcover copy of your book upon request.

Truth and service is critical to the success of any company and my company lives by those two core values. If you prefer to do it yourself, and are choosing your own editor, then I suggest that you do the following once you have received the final edited draft back from your editor. After you have gone through your final draft with your editor, I highly recommend one final process that I have already touched on briefly. This is also going to connect with the audiobook chapter that we will cover later in this book.

If you are going to do it yourself, narrate, and record the audiobook version of your book then it also serves as one final opportunity to proofread your book. This tends to be the best way to read a final proof and is a method I have used for my books. For my books, I have at least three people read it to catch errors after the final edit, but no matter what, you will always find errors. That's part of being human. I found a few minor errors in all my books while proofreading. Most of the errors found while proofreading range between five to ten small spelling or grammatical errors per book. It's going to happen and the best way to catch those final errors is to read the book aloud yourself.

You also need to decide whether you want to record the audiobook for your first book. I chose not to and did a royalty share agreement on Audible. The royalty share agreement is when you hire someone else to narrate your book. Audible has many different narrators and they will audition for you. That way you can choose the voice that you prefer. This is a service that we will help clients with, through our Done For You Publishing Service as we have worked with Audible on all our audiobooks.

Typically, the royalty for making your audiobook exclusive to Audible is forty percent. If your book is non-exclusive to Audible your royalty drops to twenty-five percent, but you can sell the audiobook yourself or give it away to build your email list.

When you enter a royalty share agreement with a narrator, you split the forty percent exclusive royalty with them. You will get twenty percent and your narrator gets twenty percent. You will also split evenly any bounties that you receive. I will go into bounties in more detail later in this book. Twenty percent of something is better than forty percent of nothing and you are guaranteed to make a profit with your first audiobook that is sold.

If you end up doing a royalty share agreement and have a narrator record the audiobook for you, then I still recommend reading the book aloud for one final proofread. You will be amazed how many small errors you find. Even with having multiple people proofread your book, after having it edited, no book will be perfect.

I had a client who had two editors and still found errors after giving it one final proofread. Proofreading it one final time is an easy process. If you plan to read it aloud, I would suggest either reading it aloud to yourself or read it to a family member or friend.

You do not have to read out the entire book in one sitting. I would recommend reading one chapter in the morning and another chapter in the evening. If you do this for a few days, then you will have everything read within a week.

You can also read all the front matter in one morning session and then read all the back matter in the evening out loud. The front matter will be your disclaimer, dedication, back-end offer with speaking, coaching, or online course, and usually a gift like an audiobook version of your book or a chapter of an upcoming book to give away in exchange for the reader's email address to join your list. We will cover the front and back matter later in the book.

The best part of reading it one chapter at a time is that you can correct any minor errors very quickly. The errors that you find in the proof will be minor with a misspelled word, or grammar error showing up possibly once or twice in a chapter.

Once you have written your second book, I do recommend recording the audiobook yourself and I will go more into detail about that process in our audiobook chapter. I did want to share with you some of the information about audiobooks in this chapter as it connects with the editing process. In my view, there is no better way to proofread your book then recording the audiobook version yourself.

When you find the right editor, I recommend building a long-term relationship with them. The more you work with the same person, the better the editing becomes as they get to know your writing style. Devin has done an incredible job with not only the edits, but also with keeping my tone and message.

Once the editing process is completed, it is then time to move on to getting your book formatted.

Chapter 8 Formatting

Once your final draft is complete, edited, and proofread then you will need to convert your book to MOBI format for Kindle. Fiverr and Upwork have many freelancers who will convert your word file to MOBI. You can also do it yourself with a program called Scrivener to format your book in both Kindle and Paperback.

I have Scrivener, but do not use it because I prefer my final draft to be converted to Kindle through outsourcing as many things can go wrong with MOBI conversions. Scrivener does have a learning curve, but other author friends of mine love it once they get used to it. My preference is to write my books in Microsoft Word, as that is the process I'm most comfortable with. When you are writing your book, you want the process to be as welcoming as possible.

If your book has multiple pictures, then the conversion does cost a little more. My travel books have many pictures so those conversions do cost more as the pictures must be compressed for the Kindle version.

Formatting to Kindle is a process that I prefer to outsource. I would recommend that you outsource at least your first book to a freelancer. If you want to use Scrivener or another program to format your book, then do what you feel is best for you. With my clients, I always want to make the writing and publishing of your first book as easy as possible as there are many moving parts in a book launch, especially when it is the launch of your first book.

We have an excellent formatter on our team who will format your book to both Kindle and paperback. The process typically takes a total of 14 days to get everything done. The best part is that you give me your draft and we take care of everything else for you.

To find out more about our services go to www.GetPublishedSystem.com and click on the services tab.

Chapter 9 Create a Book Description that Sells

The book description is also known as your sales copy. This is what will help sell your book. The goal of your book description should be to help the reader identify a problem that you will help solve. There is a great article from Bestselling Author, Kevin Kruse, which explains how to write sales copy that I highly recommend - you can check it out here. I came upon this resource while my third book, Positivity Attracts was getting ready to launch.

For my first book, Eat Less and Move More, I researched many top authors and looked at their styles. After looking at many book descriptions, I came up with the following for Eat Less and Move More.

Eat Less and Move More: My Journey shows you how you can **change your lifestyle** *without spending long hours in the gym and without starving yourself while enjoying cheat meals.*

On May 2, 2011, I received my wake-up call. I was 336 pounds, had borderline type 2 diabetes, and was recently recovered from both bronchitis and pneumonia. My bad eating habits and lifestyle choices were making me ill, but I was too wrapped up in what I was doing to spot the signs let alone to do anything about it. **That day I found myself in the doctor's office and was told that I might not be around in 5-10 years if I didn't change my**

lifestyle. That was my wake-up call. Luckily I got a second chance.

That day I realized that <u>life is short and precious</u> and I made a decision that I was going to do things differently. I decided to change my life so that I could **live life to the fullest** and **eat less and move more**.

What I decided to create for myself was:

• A healthy lifestyle that **I could be proud of**
• The **mental freedom** to live the life of my dreams
• The **freedom of good health** to do the things I love and to be with the people who matter most to me

And now I want to help you do the same.

After all, deciding to start your journey to **eat less and move more** is something you do because you have a vision of a better life for you and your family. **It's your chance to take control and live life on your terms**. And done right *it will give you* the mental freedom and the freedom of good health to do the things you love, when you want to do them and <u>with</u> the people who matter most in your life.

Eat Less and Move More will show you how to create an improved you that gives you the time to work on your own passions in life. It will also show you the mistakes that I made and what I did when I gained over half of the weight back. I also tell my story throughout the book of working in the corporate world and eventually leaving that world to pursue a career in teaching as my weight and career were connected.

In short, losing weight and keeping the weight off is not a

temporary change but a lifestyle choice by choosing to **eat less and move more.**

Eat Less and Move More shows you how you can easily start your own **journey towards a healthier lifestyle** – a lifestyle that you can be proud of <u>and</u> achieve both **mental freedom** and **freedom of good health.**

But more than this, Eat Less and Move More explores what it means to live a truly happy and fulfilled life – to *really live the life of your dreams and pursue what you love.* It encourages you to examine your own motivations and desires in order to **determine your path in life.**

To get access to the bonus materials and resources (all for FREE), be sure to visit:

www.BrodieEDU.com

It was not bad for my first launch, but after reading Kevin's article, I changed my approach for sales copy and created the following sales copy for Eat Less and Move More. I made these changes in late November 2015. One of the best things about Kindle is that you can change and update your book and change your book description whenever you want to.

Here is the new and improved sales copy.

Eat Less and Move More: My Journey shows how you can **change your mindset** and **improve your physical and mental health.**

What if a few new habits could improve your personal health? What if you could increase your health and happiness with a few simple steps? Imagine waking up in the morning feeling healthy and happy and ready to take on the day.

Amazon bestselling author, Paul G. Brodie, in his first book, covers multiple ways to improve your physical and mental health.

Here are a few things that you will get out of Eat Less and Move More.

In this book, you will learn.

- How to learn to Listen to Your Body
- How to take a Leap of Faith and Follow Your Dreams
- How to respond when your body gives you a Wakeup Call
- How to Eat Less and Move More
- How to respond if you gain weight after an initial weight loss
- How to create a healthy environment by Eating Clean
- How to Change Your Lifestyle at any age

- How to utilize Healthy Eating Habits in your everyday life
- How to enjoy Cheat Meals without feeling guilty
- BONUS: Daily Food Lists for what Paul has utilized to lose over sixty pounds and current food items that he eats to continue to live a healthy lifestyle

Buy this book NOW to increase your personal, physical and mental health

Pick up your copy today by clicking the BUY NOW button at the top of this page!

As you can see, I made a much better effort in identifying a problem for the reader and offering solutions. In addition, I added two calls to action at the end of the sales copy by telling the reader to buy now. Calls to action may sound basic, but they do work.

When you write your book description, remember that the first sentence that you write is the big promise. This is what the reader will get out of your book. With Eat Less and Move More the first sentence was change your mindset and improve your physical and mental health.

Once you have written your first sentence with the big promise, you will want to follow with two additional benefits of buying your book. Using "what if" and "imagine" statements are great ways to start the two additional benefits.

The book description needs to describe the content of your book with benefits to the reader. Another thing you can do is offer bonuses in the description. In my Maui books, I offer a free travel guide as one of the bonuses.

As you approach the end of your book description, you want to restate the big promise again. With Eat Less and Move More I added buy this book NOW to increase your personal physical and mental health.

At the end of the book description, you want to close them with BUY NOW. Here is how I close Eat Less and Move More, pick up your copy today by clicking the BUY NOW button at the top of this page.

Once you have completed your sales copy you will need to have it converted to html so your book description will stand out. With html you can bold and highlight words, increase font size, and underline words. I found a freelancer on Fiverr who converted my sales copy for five dollars. Once you get the file back, it will be in a txt file. I used a freelancer to convert my text to html for my first three launches. By the end of the third launch, I learned enough about html that I have created the html book descriptions myself going forward.

At this point, you will want to go to Amazon and to Author Central. In Author Central, you can add your personal information with an author bio and pictures. When you are ready to upload your book, you will have the option to add your sales copy in the book description. With the html code, the sales copy will stand out and you will have the ability to bold words to help grab the reader's attention.

Chapter 10 Creating Your Author Biography

As I mentioned in chapter 9, you will want to create an author biography on Amazon and in your book. I recommend creating two biographies. One will be a shorter biography for Amazon in their Author Central area. The second will be a longer biography that you can include in the back of your book.

Here is an example of the Author biography I use on Amazon.

"Quick and inexpensive reads for self-improvement, a healthier lifestyle, and book publishing"

Twelve-time Amazon bestselling author, Paul Brodie believes that books should be inexpensive, straightforward, direct, and not have a bunch of fluff.

Each of his books were created to solve problems including living a healthy lifestyle, increasing motivation, improving positive thinking, traveling to amazing destinations, and helping authors write, publish and market their books to a #1 bestseller.

What makes Paul's books different is his ability to explain complex ideas and strategies in a simple, accessible way that you can implement immediately.

Paul is lifelong learner and educator and earned an M.A. in Teaching from Louisiana College and B.B.A. in Management from the University of Texas at Arlington.

In his spare time he loves to read and write books, travel (especially to Maui and Las Vegas), and is an avid sports fan.

He resides in Arlington, TX and can be reached at Brodie@BrodieConsultingGroup.com and www.BrodieEDU.com for speaking, coaching, and consulting opportunities.

Want to know more? Then scroll down the page and check out the different eBooks (also available in paperback and audiobook format) Paul has published...

After the ... my books are shown and is a great way to encourage the reader to check out your books. This bio is short and to the point.

Here is an example of what I include in the back of my paperback books and in the About the Author section and in the back matter on my books and includes my professional picture. The bio is a lot longer and covers more of my background.

About the Author

Paul Brodie the CEO of Brodie Consulting Group, which specializes in book publishing and coaching clients on how to publish and market their books. He is also the President of BrodieEDU, an education consulting firm that specializes in giving motivational, business, publishing, and leadership seminars for universities and corporations.

Brodie left teaching in June 2017 after serving as an educator in multiple roles since 2008. He served as a Special Education Teacher from 2014-2017 in the Hurst-Euless-Bedford ISD (2014-2016) and Fort Worth ISD (2016-2017) while working specifically with special needs children who had Autism. In 2014-2015 he also served as the head tennis coach and lead the school to a district championship and an undefeated season.

From 2011-2014, Brodie served as a Grant Coordinator for the ASPIRE program in the Birdville Independent School District. As coordinator, he created instructional and enrichment programming for over 800 students and 100 parents in the ASPIRE before and after school programs. He also served on the Board of Directors for the Leadership Development Council, Inc. from 2005-2014 with leading the implementation of educational programming in low cost housing.

From 2008-2011, he was a highly successful teacher in Arlington, TX where he taught English as a Second Language. Brodie turned a once struggling ESL program into one of the top programs in the school district. Many of his students moved on to journalism, AVID, art classes, and many students exited the ESL program entirely.

Teaching methods during his career as an educator included daily writing practice, flash cards, picture cards, academic relays, music, movies, and short educational videos including the alphabet and sight words. Additional strategies included graphic novels paired with movie versions of the novels, games, cultural celebrations, and getting parents involved in their children's education. Brodie's approach has been called unconventional but very effective, revolutionary, and highly engaging. His students have always shown great improvement with both academics and behavior throughout the school year and he was honored to teach such an amazing and diverse group of students during his career as an educator.

Previously, Brodie spent many years in the corporate world and decided to leave a lucrative career in the medical field to follow his passion and transitioned into education. Prior to working in the medical field, he worked for Enterprise Rent-A-Car after receiving his Bachelor's Degree and for Savitz Research during his high school and college years. He is very grateful for every career opportunity as each one was an avenue to learn and grow.

Brodie earned an M.A. in Teaching from Louisiana College and B.B.A. in Management from the University of Texas at Arlington. Brodie is a bestselling author and has written multiple books. He wrote his first book, Eat Less and Move More: My Journey in the summer of 2015. Brodie's goal of the book was to help those like himself who had challenges with weight. The goal of his first book was to promote not only weight loss but also health and wellness. He is also the author of Motivation 101, Positivity Attracts, Book Publishing for Beginners, The Pursuit of Happiness, Maui, Just Do It, PMA, San Diego, Book Publishing for Authors, and Champion. All eleven books (available in Kindle, Paperback, and Audiobook) are Amazon bestsellers and are based on his motivational seminars, book publishing, love of travel, and struggles with weight.

His seminars have been featured at many universities and at leadership conferences across the United States since 2005. Brodie is active in professional organizations and within the community and currently serves on the Advisory Board for Advent Urban Youth Development and as a volunteer with the Special Olympics. Paul is a proud Rotarian and is a member of the Arlington

Chamber of Commerce and the Arlington Chamber Young Professionals. He continues to be involved with The International Business Fraternity of Delta Sigma Pi and has served in many positions since 2002 including National Vice President – Organizational Development, Leadership Foundation Trustee, National Organizational Development Chair, District Director, and in many other volunteer leadership roles. He resides in Arlington, TX.

The About the Author section gives you an opportunity to share your background, education, and interests. I joined both the Arlington Chamber of Commerce and Rotary this year and included both in the About the Author section. It helps continue to build the connection and relationship between you and your reader. In addition, it also helps with adding further credibility with your background especially if you hold certifications, degree or advanced degrees, and involvement in organizations with being a Rotarian or serving on a Board of Directors.

Having both, a short and long biography, also helps when others are introducing you. I have been a guest on multiple podcasts from the Side Hustle Nation Show that is based in the United

States to Writer on the Road, which is a popular podcast in Australia. The hosts want to introduce you to their audience and the short bio is perfect for this. It is short, to the point, and does a great job with telling the audience who you are.

The longer biography adds additional credibility with your background. It also continues to build the relationship between you and the reader. Your readers may also be members of a local chamber of commerce, a member of a Fraternity, or a Rotarian.

Building connections with your readership is critical. Utilizing both author bios will help to build those relationships. As part of our publishing services, we can customize both author biographies for you if you need additional support. Are you ready to create your author biography?

To find out more about our services go to www.GetPublishedSystem.com and click on the services tab.

Chapter 11 Building Your Website

I highly recommend having a website before you launch your book, if you have not already done so. The main reason is that you need it as a place to funnel the traffic from your book. I will go into more detail during the build your readership chapter.

Building a website does not need to be difficult. You need three things. The first is a domain. My first domain was www.BrodieEDU.com. I bought the domain for $10.99 for the first year on Bluehost. The next thing you need is hosting. I bought three years of hosting on Bluehost for $160.00 in July 2015. The third thing you need is to have WordPress set up on your domain. Bluehost did this for me and they walked me through the process.

I know it sounds like a lot of work, but it is not that difficult depending on what you want. In 2015, I hired a friend with an IT background to create my website with a WordPress theme. It wasn't anything fancy, but it did the job.

The goal of your website is to have a site where readers can reach you and get your lead magnets. You can get webhosting for as little as three dollars and ninety-five cents per month through Bluehost for a three-year agreement, which adds up to around $160.00. The catch is that you do have to pay in advance, but that price point is well worth the investment.

The only other item you will need to buy regarding the hosting side of your site is to buy the domain. You should be able to purchase the domain for between six to twelve dollars per year. Bluehost offers phone support and they can walk you through the set-up process. Last fall I set up a website for my dad from scratch and they walked me through the process in less than twenty minutes.

The only other item you will need to purchase is a premium WordPress theme. Last fall, I purchased a premium theme called The7 – Responsive Multi-Purpose WordPress Theme. The theme cost me forty dollars and it was a significant upgrade over my previous website design, which was a free theme from WordPress.

Once you purchase the theme (or any premium) theme you can contact Bluehost and they can walk you through the process. It is a straightforward process and is easier than you think. If you are not comfortable with creating the website yourself, you do have an option to have Bluehost build your site for you. It is whatever you prefer, but I would recommend trying to build the site yourself if you feel comfortable with trying it.

Around a year later, I took over my website and learned about how to use WordPress. Last year I built a new and improved website with the premium theme called The7 – Responsive Multi-Purpose WordPress Theme. It is my current webpage and you can go to www.BrodieEDU.com, www.BrodieConsultingGroup.com, www.GetPublishedInfo.com, and www.GetPublishedSystem.com to check out my site. I bought three additional domains that redirect to my main site.

My website has the main page and on top has a menu. The first menu is for the main page, second menu is the about page and I have my long bio on that page. On the next menu, I have the books section where readers can access my books through direct links in Kindle, paperback, and audiobook formats. After the book menu is a speaking and keynote menu where the reader can watch a video of highlights from my public speaking engagements and set up a call with me for more information. The next menu is for a free book where they can download a free copy of my publishing book in return for them signing up for my mailing list. My services menu goes into more detail about the four different ways that we can help you get published and has a video with me talking about how we can help you. The next menu is a free webinar/Webclass that readers can sign up for. The webinar is on demand and starts every hour. Next menu is the Strategy Session where readers will see a video of me and an invitation to set up a quick strategy session so I can help them with their book. The final menu is the Podcast where my readers can get more information about my Get Published Podcast.

The speaking and keynotes, free book, services, free webinar, strategy session, and podcast pages were created through Lead Pages. They are a company that you can use to create great looking landing pages for around forty dollars per month. Lead Pages has a WordPress plugin where you can redirect the landing pages to your website and it is an easy process to follow.

My company has a strategic partner that specializes in building websites so if you do need help with getting your website built then let me know and I can get you more information.

To find out more about our services go to www.GetPublishedSystem.com and click on the services tab.

Chapter 12 Getting Reviews Quickly

Getting reviews is one of the toughest things to do as an author. For your first launch, I would suggest reaching out to friends, family, acquaintances, and Facebook friends to get honest reviews. Your goal by the first week of uploading your book to Amazon is to get at least five to ten reviews.

To build your momentum for your book launch you want to have at least ten to fifteen reviews by the end of your launch. Book reviews help Amazon potentially promote your book as a hot new release. Having many book reviews shows social proof that your book is worth buying.

Book reviews are challenging to get. You need to have multiple strategies to reach out to reviewers and you cannot be timid with asking for reviews.

I ended up contacting over 100 people for my first book launch. Out of those 100 people contacted, only 12 people submitted reviews. The good part is that once you get to know fellow authors in Facebook groups, then you are eventually able to build upon your brand and you will get more reviews. This has proven as Eat Less and Move more had 17 reviews, Motivation 101 had 22 reviews and Positivity Attracts after only a few weeks on Amazon has 33 reviews by the end of the launch phase.

For your first book, the process will be tough. People you think you can rely on will most likely let you down. One of the strategies I would recommend is what I did for my third book, Positivity Attracts.

I found that uploading the final version of the PDF file to Dropbox and then sending the link to fellow author pals and a few friends that are always helpful and leave reviews for me on both Amazon and Goodreads was successful. You will want reviews on both pages, as Goodreads readers can be very critical about books. They are very passionate and tend to consider very good books to be only 3 to 4 stars while Amazon readers will typically grade your book as 4 to 5 stars.

Be sure to send follow up messages to your potential reviewers too. I would recommend sending out the advance copies a week before you upload your book to Amazon. Once you upload to Amazon, send a follow up message to ask if they had a chance to read the book. Let them know that the book is uploaded and available for 99 cents and that you could really use their support by downloading a copy and leaving you a review.

I have found this to work well, but I would not recommend contacting the same person more than four times.

Another tactic that you can do is creating a book launch group on Facebook. You can invite your Facebook friends to the group and post regularly in the group. I had a Facebook group for my third launch. I would say that I received fifteen reviews in my launch group for Positivity Attracts, which was helpful.

Another way to add social proof to your book launch is utilizing editorial reviews. You will use parts of reviews from people who leave you reviews. Editorial reviews will show up on your book page before all other reviews.

You can create editorial reviews by setting up your Amazon author central page at the following website https://authorcentral.amazon.com. Do not set up the page until after your book is live on Amazon. It is an easy process to follow. I am going to show you examples of editorial reviews from my second Maui book that was published in April 2018.

Editorial Reviews

"ALOHA! If you always enjoy or have never experienced your own personal Hawaiian adventure, this is your guide, from landing to leaving and everything in between. Even if you are an expert island hopper, Paul's detailed descriptions, directions and diversions will save you time and treasure by detailing the best How to, Where to and When to do it all."
- David

"What I like about the book. He offers remarkable tips on how to streamline your planning from airline tickets, rental car choices, and grocery purchases before even getting to the fabulous-sounding restaurants and activities. The wonderful photos are an extra bonus. What I did not like about the book. There is no link to instantly transport me to the beautiful island."
- Sam

"I gave this book 5 stars because of the depth of information it contains. Just about any area involved in traveling to another country was covered, and the tips can be used to plan trips to other locations. For example, the differences in using an online platform and booking directly. The tip about having a Costco card is priceless

because even if there's no Costco in another location outside the US, it created an awareness that these are questions that can be asked or researched when planning your trip. Finding good food that's available outside of restaurants, like food trucks, is a great alternative. One I particularly appreciated was knowing which stores will give you cash back so as to eliminate high ATM fees for overseas transactions."
- Yvonne

"It's always been a dream of mine to enjoy a Hawaiian vacation. When my dream becomes a reality (which, after reading this book, I hope will be very soon) I'll know exactly where to go and what to do. Paul Brodie has created the perfect vacation planner - it answers all your questions and takes away the anxiety of scheduling a trip to someplace new. I also particularly enjoyed the pictures of all that delicious looking food!"
- Amazon Reader

"A succinct illustrated guide that allows you to make the most of your holiday, without wasting precious time. From booking tickets, to the best food trucks on the island, Paul has got your covered. I love that the book also includes a chapter on where to see the best sunsets. Before

you set off for your Maui break, be sure to grab this book to optimize your stay!"
- Susan

"This book certainly whetted my appetite for holidaying in Maui. Glorious beaches and sunsets as well as delicious food and even turtles. Maui here I come! This is another lovely travel book by Paul Brodie, which I thoroughly enjoyed. Highly recommended for real travelers as well as the armchair kind."
- Amazon Reader

"The main thing I want to stress about this book is that Paul covers the smallest of details that can honestly make a huge difference in the success or failure of a vacation. He doesn't overlook a single step and shares valuable tips not only about typical food and sights to see, but practical ways to save money and stretch your dollar so you can enjoy much more! I really considered choosing Maui as my next vacation spot after reading this book."
- Amazon Reader

"This book offers practical tips that will both save you money and make sure your trip to Maui is as enjoyable as it should be. The author's thorough research will definitely save you a lot of time and

hassle. If you're a foodie and look for places to eat, you won't be disappointed either. So, if you plan to visit Maui in the near future, don't forget to bring a copy of this book with you."
- Meurisse

Having editorial reviews will help with adding social proof to your book page. Getting reviews is a tedious and time-consuming process. You want to reach out to as many people as possible, especially for your first book launch. Remember that your goal is to have at least ten to fifteen reviews by the end of your book launch.

You can do it! Persistence is key to a successful book launch.

Chapter 13 Marketing Your Book Launch

During the launch process, there are two parts to the marketing side of launching your book. The first part is the free launch strategy, which will help get your book into the hands of as many people as possible. What I first suggest, is to decide whether you want to do a four or five-day strategy for your free launch. Again, as an author who is starting out I would suggest going the free route to get your book into as many hands as possible.

After deciding whether you want to go the four or five-day route, you will want to decide on dates. My first four book launches would start on a Sunday. On Sunday morning, I created a status update on Facebook about my book being free to encourage people to check it out while free. I also post it on Twitter and Instagram.

Here is an example of what I recommend doing on a free launch as I used this strategy with my first four books. We have made changes and implemented an updated customized launch strategy that we do for our clients and students in our Book Publishing Implementation Program, but the promos listed are all good places to start for your book launch.

Sunday Day #1. BKnights Promotion (costs $5.00 on Fiverr.com)

Monday Day #2. Freebooksy Promotion (costs $80.00 on freebooksy.com). This is the best investment that you can make in my view for your free launch. This day your book is most likely to rank highest.

Tuesday Day #3. BKnights Promotion (costs $5.00 on Fiverr.com)
Typically, there are readers from Freebooksy that might not check their e-mail right away and I have always had a second day of strong downloads from Freebooksy readers. Most downloads will be in the morning.

Wednesday Day #4. No promotions.

Thursday Day #5 is the day that I decide to end the promotion and do so at 6:30 pm central time. This has the book available in prime time (7:00 to 11:00 pm) on Amazon and I want to have my book converted to paid as soon to prime time as possible.

After stopping the free launch, the book will still show up in the free rankings for a couple of hours. The book will show a 99-cent price point and it should generate sales for your book. As an example, on this strategy, after the free launch for Positivity Attracts ended, it was #1 in all its book categories and was in the top 2400 in all of Amazon Kindle once it transitioned back into the paid categories.

With the launches, I want to generate as much buzz as possible and having your book for free for a limited time helps in that process. Now that you have converted your book to 99 cents, it is time to generate traffic to your book and get as many sales as possible. I am following similar concepts from the free strategy with having the book at 99 cents for the next 4.5 days.

Thursday evening. End the free launch around 6:30 pm central time.

Day #1 Friday. No promotions. Amazon will see your book doing well and it will start to be shown in the Customers Who Bought This Item Also Bought section of Kindle Books on Amazon. The publicity gained is great for your book and should help bring in sales.

Day #2 Saturday. Reading Deals promotion. ($29.00)

Day #3 Sunday. Bargain Booksy promotion. ($25.00)

Day #4 Monday. Buck Books promotion. ($35.00)

Day #5 Tuesday. No promotions. Convert your price from 99 cents to either $2.99 or $3.99 at noon central time. If your book is over one-hundred pages, then consider $3.99 as a price point.

Sales will slip but remember that your book will be making $2.06 cents per sale instead of .35 cents at the $2.99 price point. Do not worry if things slow down for a day or two. The Amazon Algorithm will kick in and you should see your book being featured in the Customers Also Bought section of many top books. I have seen this for all my books. I checked the Buck Books daily email for the next several days and I saw my books being featured in the Customers Also Bought section every day.

The books that are promoted on Buck Books usually end up in the top 8000 at minimum in Amazon Kindle and I have seen quite a few in the top 2000 including all my books. You will most likely see your book in that section so definitely subscribe to Buck Books for their daily e-mail as it is an efficient way to track your book in that section.

CASE STUDY: MIMI EMMANUEL

I want to share with you a case study from Mimi Emmanuel. Mimi and I have worked together since early 2016. At the time, Mimi was creating her first book about book publishing. Mimi reached out to me after reading my first publishing book, as she wanted help with her branding, launch and marketing strategy. I helped Mimi with her branding, launch plan and marketing strategy and her book became a #1 bestseller.

Later in 2016 we worked together again on her biggest success yet. Mimi created her second book about book publishing. I helped Mimi again, with her branding and launch plan and her book became a #1 bestseller in multiple categories.

The results were amazing. Mimi has published four books that ranked as #1 bestsellers in over forty categories. This is what Mimi said about working with me.

"I LOVE the 'Book Publishing Implementation Program' and am so happy to have come across Paul and his teachings. He is an absolute ACE teacher and I cannot recommend his top-notch video modules and coaching sessions highly enough. The abundance of resources about writing, publishing and marketing that Paul delivers in the program is perfect for anyone who wants to become a bestselling author and take their book writing and publishing to the next level." Mimi Emmanuel

While we have touched briefly on some of the marketing in this book, we have not covered everything, as there is a lot of information, especially with marketing your book. There are several ways that we can help you have a successful book launch with a customized marketing plan with a proven system that works and will ensure that your book becomes a #1 bestseller.

First is through our Done For You Book Launch Marketing Service where we also offer our #1 bestseller guarantee. We will create a customized book launch marketing plan for you with over 20 book promo companies that includes everything that you need to have your book become a #1 bestseller. The cost of the book promos is included with the service.

Next option is through our VIP One-On-One Coaching Service where I will personally help you customize a book launch, just like I did for Billy Atwell. We have personal relationships with many of the book promo companies and will ensure through our personal connections and contact information that your book is featured on their site and their promo emails when it is time to launch your book.

In our Book Publishing Implementation Program, we dedicate two complete modules in the program to my book marketing strategy that will help you implement my own book marketing system that has taken all my books to a #1 bestseller including all my clients. We cover the exact launch sequence from the day that you upload your book to Amazon, to when to book the promos, including all the current information on who we recommend using. I also go through over 20 book promo companies that I recommend as our launch strategy has evolved into a proven system that will work for your book.

Not only do we take a deep dive into creating your own marketing plan for your book launch, I also include contact information for some of the promo companies including personal email addresses for the bookers of some of the toughest promo sites to get books on including Buck Books. The information in this chapter will be helpful in your journey, but implementation with the program and working with me will make a huge difference in the future success of your book. Do you want to be our next success story?

To find out more about our services go to www.GetPublishedSystem.com and click on the services tab.

Chapter 14 Creating Your Audiobook

Having multiple revenue streams are critical to becoming not only a successful author, but also in any business. I read an article several years ago that explained the average millionaire entrepreneur had an average of seven revenue streams. Audiobooks are another great revenue stream to have as an author.

I decided to add audiobooks to my launches starting with my second book, Motivation 101. With my first book, Eat Less and Move More, I was incredibly busy with the launch and I did not have time to get the audiobook done at the time of the launch. After the launch finished, I started to research audiobook options and found that I could do it myself.

When I started recording my own audiobooks, I bought a condenser microphone called the Blue Snowball ICE Condenser Microphone and a pop filter from Amazon. The cost was around $56.00 for both and I downloaded the Audacity program for free, which would allow me to record the book. I used that mic to record seven of my audiobooks.

In 2017, I bought a new microphone. I highly recommend it, the ATR 2100-USB Cardioid

Dynamic Microphone. Many authors use this mic to record audiobooks and many podcast hosts use the mic for their podcasts. You can buy the ATR 2100 on Amazon for around sixty-five dollars.

You will also need to reach out to your freelancer and have them convert your Kindle book cover to audiobook size. It should not cost too much and having the cover is just as important for sales as it is for a Kindle cover. Unfortunately, I found this out the hard way. I did not have audiobook covers ready for several weeks after both the Motivation 101 and Eat Less and Move More audiobooks were published. This was a costly mistake not worth repeating.

For Motivation 101, I wanted to have an audiobook available at the time of the launch for two reasons. The first was to have the additional revenue stream and the second was to use it as a lead magnet.

I recorded the book over two weekends. There is a lot of work that goes into recording it yourself, so you need to decide if you want to take on that responsibility or work a royalty agreement out with having someone else record it for you. I have gone both routes.

As I mentioned earlier in the book, there are three different royalty rates with Audible. If you decide to make the book exclusive to Audible then you will get a forty percent royalty. The royalty percentage does change to twenty percent if you do a royalty share agreement and have a narrator record the audiobook for you. They also will upload the audiobook to Audible for you. The other royalty rate is twenty-five percent and happens when you make the audiobook non-exclusive to Audible. That means that you keep the audiobook rights and can sell it yourself or give it away.

I did that with Motivation 101 and I gave away the audiobook version to add people to my email list. By choosing that route, I added over one thousand three hundred subscribers to my email list and was well worth doing.

Over two weekends in 2015, I recorded Motivation 101; it took me two to three hours each weekend to record the audio. It was not an easy process, but I did learn a few things that I will cover.

My first suggestion is to record the smaller chapters first. This also includes the intro, foreword (if you have one), contact information, and some of the smaller chapters. Leave the longer chapters for the following weekend. You will make mistakes and you will have to re-record chapters again. It is a frustrating process at times, but it does get better.

When I recorded Positivity Attracts, it was much easier and took me four hours instead of five to six hours. I do highly recommend finding a small room to record in. Do not have the air conditioning or heating on, you want the room as quiet as possible. I also recommend having the mic on at least three to four large hardback books and have the mic six inches from your face. This will help in case your computer fan is a little loud. You will always want to speak into the mic.

Another option is to buy a microphone suspension mic clip adjustable boom studio scissor arm stand. You can find it on Amazon for around twelve dollars. Once you receive the stand all you need to do is use the adjustable mount to mount it to your desk. If you plan to record a lot of audiobooks or online courses, it is perfect, as it will only take you a few seconds to set up for recording.

Once you have recorded a chapter I highly recommend that you listen to it immediately. If it sounds good and you are happy with it, go to the next chapter. Continue the process for those two weekends until your audiobook is complete. I also recommend taking a five to ten-minute break every thirty to forty-five minutes. You will want to get some water and possibly some hot tea, because your vocal chords will get tired. In addition, when recording, you will also want to pause before speaking at the start of each chapter for two to three seconds and then start to speak. At the end of each chapter, also leave two to three seconds of silence.

Once your recording is complete, you will want to send the files to someone who can edit and remaster your recording. In audiobook recordings, ACX wants there to be a slight gap at the beginning and end of each chapter. The two to three seconds of silence is that gap. Your freelancer can make this flow very smoothly, but you do need to leave that space.

For my first book, Eat Less and Move More, I decided that I did not want to record it myself. My other books were around ten thousand words and Eat Less and Move More was almost twice as long. I chose to do a royalty share agreement and had a narrator on ACX do the recording. This option only gives you twenty percent commission as the narrator also gets twenty percent as well. Since I did not want to record it, I felt that twenty percent of something was better than forty percent of nothing.

It is an easy process as you submit the information on ACX and narrators will audition for you. After listening to ten auditions, I chose my narrator and he recorded the book within five days. The narrator also uploads the audiobook to ACX, which is great. It was available on Amazon, Audible, and iTunes within two weeks.

You will also be eligible for the fifty-dollar bounty program from Audible. Audible/ACX offers a fifty-dollar bounty each time an audiobook produced by ACX is the first purchase by a new subscriber to Audible. You will receive the bounty after the new subscriber has completed 61 days of membership. You will receive the full fifty dollars regardless if your audiobook is exclusive at 40 percent or non-exclusive at 25 percent. If you have done a royalty-share agreement then you will get twenty-five dollars and the narrator of your book through the royalty-share agreement will get the other twenty-five dollars. The bounty system is a great additional revenue stream and I have collected fifteen full bounties and two additional bounties through the royalty-share agreement since starting this journey three years ago.

One other thing about ACX is that the audiobook will most likely not be ready in time for your launch. You cannot upload the audiobook until your Kindle eBook is available on Amazon. At that point, you can upload the audiobook. Again, the audiobooks are a long-term investment. You will not make a ton of money starting out and might only make 10-20 dollars on average for the first couple of months. It should pay off long term.

Another great benefit of recording it yourself is that you will find errors in your book that you may not have caught initially. No matter how awesome your editor is (and I have an AMAZING editor) there will be mistakes that do not get caught. Recording the audiobook aloud will help you find the other mistakes. I have found at least ten errors with both Motivation 101 and Positivity Attracts while recording the audiobooks.

If you are going to record an audiobook yourself, I would recommend recording the audiobook first, before having your book converted to Kindle. For my books, I use the Microsoft Word version of my book to record the audiobooks and then made corrections to any errors found to the file while recording the audiobook; I have the final draft converted to Kindle and then paperback.

If you live in the Dallas/Fort Worth Metroplex and are wanting to record it yourself then please feel free to contact me. One of my strategic partners is an audio genius and has a service where he will personally help you record your audiobook in his recording studio. There is an investment involved, but if you are wanting to record it yourself in a professional studio then I highly recommend looking into it.

Before we move to the next chapter, I want to share the feedback that I received from one of my students who graduated from our Book Publishing Implementation Program. I am sharing her feedback in this chapter as one of Hillary's goals as an author is to record and narrate her audiobooks.

"I read Paul Brodie's book, Book Publishing for Beginners, and his style of writing immediately put me at ease. He not only provided well-thought out step-by-step instructions, insights, and behind-the-scenes knowledge about self-publishing that only someone with his experience and expertise could know, but he shared them with encouragement and a 'you can do this' attitude. Because of Paul's in-depth knowledge

and positive attitude when I realized I needed a real-life coach to show me how to market my books and create audiobooks, I signed up for his Book Publishing Implementation Program. It was the best decision! With Paul by my side, I'm no longer afraid to record my first audiobook, and I know my books will get into the hands of my readers." Hillary Tubin, Author of Boys and Books

Chapter 15 Building Your Readership

Now it is time to begin building your audience if you have not already done so. When you release your book, you will have traffic coming to it. Your Kindle will have traffic from Amazon, your audiobook traffic will come from Amazon and Audible, and your paperback traffic will come from Amazon and CreateSpace. Your goal is to funnel as much of that traffic as possible to your list to build your own audience.

When I first heard the term funnel, I was not clear on what it meant. The goal of the term funnel is to move the readers who buy your books on Amazon, Audible, and CreateSpace to your email list.

Your goal is to funnel as many readers of your books as possible to your email list. That way, you can contact them yourself since Amazon is not going to give you the names of the readers who buy your books. The best way to get the readers funneled to your list is to give them something of value through having a lead magnet.

MailChimp is the list service that I currently use. It is free for your first two thousand subscribers. After you reach two thousand subscribers, you must pay for the service. MailChimp is good, but they do not offer an auto responder option for the free service. An auto responder is where you can draft a series of email messages over a span of time that a new subscriber to your list will receive when they sign up to your list. Originally, I was going to change my email provider from Mailchimp to AWeber once I went over two thousand subscribers, but decided to stay with Mailchimp.

I also have Drip as it does include an autoresponder. The service costs $49.00 per month for up to twenty-five hundred subscribers. I use Drip specifically with our on-demand Webclass to send reminders and for the follow up sequence once the Webclass is over.

As a new author starting out, I highly recommend starting with Mailchimp as it does take time to build your email list. It took me eighteen months to get over two thousand subscribers. Going with Mailchimp to get started is a great option, especially while the service is free for the first two thousand subscribers.

Once you get over two thousand subscribers, I would recommend looking at several services. AWeber and Infusionsoft are two email providers worth looking at. You also might want to look at Click Funnels. Their premium package is expensive at two hundred ninety-seven dollars per month, but that is for an unlimited number of subscribers.

With Mailchimp, AWeber, and Infusionsoft you will pay more per month as your list grows. That is why I highly recommend using Mailchimp while getting started.

Another benefit of Mailchimp is that it is easy to use, has a high delivery rate and will reach your readers. Sometimes AWeber and Infusionsoft have challenges at times with delivering emails. It doesn't happen often from what I have heard from other authors, but things do happen. Mailchimp is a lot more reliable and is one of the main reasons that I continue to use the service, even though I now pay a monthly fee.

Once you have decided on your email service and website it is time to think about how you are going to build your audience, otherwise known as your subscribers. Your subscriber list is your tribe so to speak. Your subscribers on your list have a connection to you through your book and are interested in what you are offering. Building a large reader list is critical to an author's success and to their revenue streams.

The first thing you need to do is decide on what type of lead magnet that you want to give away. Lead magnets are what you will be giving away to your reader to get them to join your list.

I use Lead Pages (costs thirty-seven dollars per month for the standard plan) to offer freebies to get readers. For that price, you get virtually unlimited pages that you can create. You also do not need your own website as Lead Pages host the pages on their page.

If you do have your own website, you can redirect the page to your website. For example, my free Motivation 101 audiobook is hosted on Lead Pages, but is also available at www.BrodieEDU.com/FreeAudioBook.

I would suggest Lead Pages if you are starting out as the lower cost might be a better option compared to Click Funnels. In 2017, I added Click Funnels due to wanting to accept secure online payments. The service is more expensive, but they do offer the best landing pages around and the easiest to create. You can create a landing page in less than a minute. Click Funnels costs ninety-seven dollars a month, but with the secure payment option was worth the upgrade.

Both Lead Pages and Click Funnels offer options to create links on your own website through WordPress plugins and are easy to install. It looks better having the landing pages link to your own website and are easier to promote in your books and through external links that you can share on social media through Facebook, Twitter, and Instagram.

My first freebie was created for the launch of my first book, Eat Less and Move More in August 2015. I wrote both Eat Less and Move More and version 1 of my second book, Motivation 101. Version 1 of Motivation 101 had my old cover that I wrote about earlier in the book and was edited, but was not a final copy.

It was a great lead magnet as I got over 100 readers to sign up to my list. In September 2015, I edited the lead page and changed out the free book of Motivation 101 to the free audiobook. I finalized Motivation 101 with a new cover and a final round of edits and launched the eBook on Amazon in mid-September for an early October launch.

The audiobook of Motivation 101 was my new lead magnet and did well. Since adding the audiobook as a lead magnet, we have added over one-thousand three hundred subscribers to my email list through giving away the audiobook.

A strategy that I have learned from Kevin Kruse, is to make offers for each chapter of a book. You identify a theme in the chapter and offer something that correlates, and then have all the items in one bundle. You will notice that strategy in this book with offering free access to my Get Published Facebook Community. What I realized is that there was a lot of additional information that I felt could be covered in the Facebook group and would be another great place to connect.

Having multiple offers in a book (like this one) greatly increases the probability of funneling the reader to your list. One of my most important goals is not only to build a great list of readers, but also to always give people a lot of value for free. At times, I will offer a service, such as my free Get Published Webclass, but the main things I will be offering is freebies and free advanced copies of my books. That way, there is always value for the readers as I hope that many of you will take advantage of one of the offers in this book.

If you do want to know what item has brought me the most subscribers it is by far the audiobook giveaway. The Motivation 101 audiobook has added over one-thousand three hundred subscribers to my list and that number has grown every day. Another thing to look at is the statistics that both Lead Pages and Click Funnels offer for their landing pages.

The statistics will show your conversion rate. Your conversion rate is the percent of people that go to your page and download your offer. Typically, any conversion rate over thirty percent is good.

I have given away a variety of items in my books ranging from travel guides (thirty-four percent conversion), to an author resource guide (forty-two percent conversion) to motivational guides (conversion rate of thirty three percent on average).

My Motivation 101 audiobook conversion rate is forty-three percent and is a great conversion rate. Audiobooks are also very popular and is a great way to promote back-end offerings that we will cover in the next chapter as several of my clients contacted me initially after listening to the audiobook version of one of my books. All those statistics are through the end of 2017.

You can also offer sneak previews of your upcoming books by offering the first chapter. Another option is to record the first chapter of your next book in audiobook format and offer that as a lead magnet.

In 2018, we changed all our lead magnet landing pages in Lead Pages. It increased our conversion rate to as high as seventy percent for some of our lead magnets. As a new bonus, we offer a personal walkthrough to anyone who signs up for any of our coaching and publishing services to help them with their landing pages as it has proven to be a game changer.

Go to www.Facebook.com and type "Get Published" in the search bar to join me, current, and aspiring authors in my Get Published Facebook Community to get additional support with building your readership.

Chapter 16 Making Revenue on the Back-End

Back-end products are going to be where you make the most revenue from your book launch. It is the reason why you want to funnel traffic from Amazon by building your audience through your subscriber email list. This is also why we want to get your book into the hands of as many people as possible and is why I highly recommend giving your book away for free for part of your book launch.

The whole point of building your list is to be able to not only give value to your readers, but also to offer products and services otherwise known as back-end products. I offer four different services including our Book Publishing Implementation Program, One-On-One VIP Coaching, Done For You Book Publishing Service, and our Done For You Book Launch Marketing Service that includes our #1 bestseller guarantee.

The main coaching offer is my Book Publishing Implementation Program. It is for people who want to learn how to write, publish, and market their book with our proven system. The program includes ten video modules and five live group video coaching calls with me and was created over the summer of 2017. As a new bonus, the five-live group coaching calls have been expanded to twenty-six calls over the next twelve months. The implementation program is the ideal system if you want to learn how to how to write, publish, and market your book to a #1 bestseller.

The program is offered at the end of my free Get Published Webclass. In the Webclass, I teach a lot of great content that helps people write, publish, and market their book regardless of whether they decide to join my program.

I have always believed in offering the best content possible and in the training, we teach amazing content for the first forty-five minutes. In the final fifteen minutes, I go over the offer as we do offer a significant discount for anyone who joins the program during the webinar.

The Book Publishing Implementation Program is amazing and I am very proud of the success that my student Authors have achieved through the program.

The program offers ten video modules that cover the entire book publishing process including:

- Outlining, writing, and finishing your draft
- Finding the best book cover
- Creating a great book description

- Uploading your book
- How to get reviews
- My entire book marketing system and is the same exact system that I have used to launch all my books to a #1 bestseller and all my clients
- How to maximize revenue streams on the front-end with having your book available in Kindle, Paperback, and Audiobook formats for your launch (also includes how-to guides)
- How to build your audience
- How to offer back-end products to maximize revenue from public speaking, online courses, and coaching

Multiple bonuses are offered including:

- Lifetime Access to the Book Publishing Implementation Program Private Facebook group
- Sixty-minute One-On-One strategy session with Paul
- Lifetime access to Replays of Live Group Coaching Calls
- Lifetime access to All Ten Video Modules Including All Updates
- Two Bonus Modules

- Live Group Coaching Calls with Paul extended to 26 calls over 12 months
- Autographed Paperback Copy of Paul's Publishing Book
- Invitation to be a guest on my Get Published Podcast to promote your book when it is released

We also offer a personal walkthrough to anyone who signs up for any of our coaching and publishing services to help them with their landing pages as it has proven to be a gamechanger. With the program, the most important part is that it isn't done for you or do it yourself. It is done with you as we implement together and that is the secret sauce when you choose to work with me. If you have the time to invest an hour a week to learn how to implement our proven system then I highly recommend that you check it out.

We also offer a 30-Day Money Back Guarantee so the investment in the program is risk free. In the program, we take a deep dive into each area of book publishing and the weekly modules average between thirty-five to fifty-five minutes for each module. The modules are sent out on a weekly basis for ten weeks and you also get two bonus modules.

We also have five live group coaching calls with me during the program where I answer any questions that you have about the book writing, publishing and marketing process with your book. The calls are a lot of fun and we have great time when our group gets together. I also offered a new bonus with extending the calls from five to twenty-six over the next twelve months. That bonus alone grew our student enrollment significantly with the additional support throughout the next 12 months to help you get published.

I offer public speaking and keynotes and have an offer in the front matter of each of my seminar series books. Originally, my goal as an author was to increase business with my motivational speaking services and it made a significant difference where I can now charge $3,000 on average and up to $5,000 depending on the event. I mainly speak at college campuses, but our corporate business has also increased. Those increases have happened due to offering additional seminars that expanded from motivational seminars to leadership and publishing seminars.

Offering public speaking is a great way to expand your business. Having a paperback version of your book will make all the difference in increasing your public speaking business. Your book will make you an authority in your area of expertise. I give away paperback versions of my book during seminars at leadership conferences as lead magnets in return for having audience members fill out interest forms to bring me to their campus or business. It works as I typically have at least fifteen to twenty-five leads at the end of every seminar that I receive through giving away the paperback book, which is typically the book version of the seminar.

CASE STUDY: BRADLEY MILES

I want to share with you a case study from Bradley Miles. Bradley reached out to me in 2017 after listening to the audiobook version of my first publishing book. He needed help with the revenue stream part of his book launch with both having a paperback version of his book and how to position the book into speaking opportunities.

We came up with a game plan to make Bradley an authority in Venture Capital through his book, #Break Into VC. Bradley also requested my help with his branding, launch plan and marketing strategy. We set a very specific marketing strategy, with both the free launch and 99-cent launch before the price increased to the regular price. The book was also available in paperback so he could sell them through CreateSpace and purchase copies directly from CreateSpace to give away at his speaking events.

The results were amazing as Bradley had his first bestselling book one month after graduating from college. He makes significant revenue on the back-end from speaking engagements across the United States thanks to the success of his book. This is what Bradley had to say about working with me.

"I was a student with a dream of writing and one day becoming a bestselling author. It seemed like a dream a lifetime away, but after learning from Paul, I

understood the importance of writing what I know and how to achieve bestseller status on Amazon.

After writing about my journey towards a career in venture capital, my book #BreakIntoVC turned into a bestseller in the venture capital category and has created a tremendous amount of opportunities for me.

Since writing my book I have lectured at Harvard, Wharton, Columbia, USC and many other schools. Paul's advice about book publishing and the power of multiple revenue streams are invaluable and I owe a lot to Paul's coaching." Bradley Miles

Becoming a Book Publishing Coach in early 2016 has made me a considerable amount of revenue for me on the back-end and the coaching combined with my motivational speaking events enabled me to leave my job as a Special Education Teacher in June 2017. This was achieved while teaching full-time, so there is time to build a business for you and a catalog of back-end products that you can offer to your readership while still working full-time.

One thing I want to make clear about coaching is that you need to decide on the niche that you want to coach in if you have not already done so. Different niches include life coaching, health and wellness, spirituality, travel, real estate, helping people relocate to a new area, or book publishing. You do not want to make your coaching too general. You want it to be specific as possible to be successful. That is why I chose book publishing as my niche because I developed a proven system that works and more importantly could use the system to help other people in their author journey.

Webinars are another great way to promote your product or service. I will freely admit that I completely screwed up my first webinar product. I created a lead page and promoted it actively in the release of Motivation 101. I was selling a three-part webinar for $49.99 (which was 50 percent off the $99.99 price point). It would address three key components from the book with the first one covering Our Greatest Opponent. It failed miserably!

What I should have done was offered a FREE webinar and then sold my coaching service on the back-end. I would have most likely made a lot more revenue with that initial webinar and it was a lesson learned. Sometimes products will sell well, and sometimes they will fail.

Another back-end product that is worth considering is creating video courses. Creating an online course is a way for you to create content and have students sign up. It does take a lot of work to set up, but it is a great opportunity to make significant passive income as once your product is uploaded then you market it and start to build your business. My goal is to create multiple smaller courses in the future including how to create your own audiobook, how to become a professional speaker, and other courses.

All you need to do is purchase an account on Vimeo.com where you can upload up to five gigs of data per week. The initial account to get started costs sixty dollars per year and their business account costs twenty dollars per month. I upgraded my account to a business account due to the growth of my Book Publishing Implementation Program.

To record the content, you can use the microphone that I recommended earlier in this book and buy video capture software. I use Debut Video Capture Software. It cost me twenty-five dollars for the license and the instructions are easy to follow. To create an online course, you can create between six to ten video modules. You can create power point slides through Microsoft Office or use Open Office for each module. Once the slides are created, you can use Debut to record your narration for the module. Use the information that you create in the slides and then expand on the information when recording the narration.

The potential with online courses is to make hundreds if not thousands of dollars a month, but it does take time. The best advice I can give to any author is to be patient. This is a marathon, not a sprint. It is a process and it takes time.

Rome was not built in a day, and it does take patience as you slowly build your back-end offerings. Therefore, I want you to be clear on what you want to get out of publishing your own book. Is it the opportunity to do public speaking? Is it to begin or expand your professional coaching? Do you want to create an online course? Are you wanting to scale your business to take it to the next level?

Go to www.Facebook.com and type "Get Published" in the search bar to join me, current, and aspiring authors in my Get Published Facebook Community to get additional support with different back-end products.

Chapter 17 Revenue Streams

In previous chapters, I have mentioned having multiple revenue streams. This is the key to becoming successful in any business and especially as an author. Having just a Kindle version of your book in my view is not enough, especially with starting out. At minimum, I highly recommend having both a Kindle and paperback version of your book ready for each book launch. Below are potential revenue streams.

Kindle Edition of your book

Paperback Edition (CreateSpace)

Audiobook (Audible/ACX)

Public Speaking

Coaching

Book Signings

Online Courses

The paperback edition of your book is essentially the modern-day business card. It is a great way to promote yourself and I highly recommend always having several copies of each of your books with you, either in your car or in your backpack, purse, etc. I also recommend reaching out to bookstores where you can ask about doing book signings. They are a great potential revenue stream. You can typically buy your books from CreateSpace in bulk (around 100 copies) for around $250.00 to $300.00. If you end up selling 100 books at a book signing then your profit margin is potentially $700.00 on one successful book signing.

One thing that I do is to have book signings at the end of my motivational seminars when speaking at university campuses or for companies. I will offer either a package deal ($1000.00 for 100 books to sign) or sell them ala cart. It is a great way to bring in additional revenue and the investment is well worth it.

I also utilize the paperback versions to warm up my leads. If I am meeting in person with a perspective client, I will bring one of my publishing books with me. At the end of the conversation, I will give them an autographed copy of my book. The book is autographed before the meeting and includes a personalized inscription about how I am looking forward to helping them and include my cell phone number below my signature. It will be one of the warmest leads that you can get as potential clients love gifts. Think about it! A book that cost 2-3 dollars could being in several thousand dollars. Not a bad return on investment. Could you imagine yourself doing that?

There are many revenue streams to utilize. These are a few helpful ideas on your journey to becoming a #1 bestselling author. Do you see how this can change your business?

Go to www.Facebook.com and type "Get Published" in the search bar to join me, current, and aspiring authors in my Get Published Facebook Community to get additional support with how to maximize revenue streams.

Chapter 18 Next Steps and Special Offer

Are you ready to get published? How will having a #1 bestseller change your life? Ready to work with me and get published with a proven system that works?

Now that we are getting near the end of this book, you should have a clear vision of where you want to go in your author journey. I want to share with you two testimonials by Billy Atwell and Sandra Joines. Both Billy and Sandra wrote forewords at the beginning of this book and they utilized and implemented our proven system for writing, publishing, and marketing their books to a #1 bestseller.

"Everyone kept telling me that I needed to write a book to establish my authority as a self-confidence coach. The problem was that I had no idea how to make that possible.

Because of Paul Brodie and his generous sharing of showing me the ropes through his coaching and video modules, I went from someone without a draft to becoming a #1 Bestselling Author in 60 days!

I was able to do this because Paul laid everything out in a clear, time-lined series of action steps that kept me focused, accountable and able to implement all that was necessary to achieve this success. He can do the same for you."

Billy Atwell, Bestselling Author of Unshakable Self-Confidence

"Paul Brodie is the guru of book publishing. He's taken a difficult, confusing, and time-consuming process and broken it down into easy-to-follow steps. Paul's Coaching and Publishing Services are a must-have for the person who dreams of becoming an author or for the seasoned author who wants to increase sales.

I feel so fortunate to have participated in his amazing Coaching Program. Mr. Brodie and his system has taken me from a published fiction author to a rock star—well, maybe not a rock star, but how does an Amazon bestselling author sound? This system works, and I highly recommend it."

Sandra Joines, Bestselling Author of Shoe in the Road

By the time that you have reached this chapter, you should have an idea about the following:

What do you want to get out of your book?

What is the title of your book?

What is the subtitle for your book?

What do you want your book cover to look like?

What will be the main ten talking points for your outline?

Will you write or speak out your book?

Once you have a clear answer for each of those questions then you will have what you need to get your first draft completed. When you are ready to start your first draft, I want you to set up a quick strategy session with me. Below is the direct appointment link to set up a call. I do have limited time slots available due to demand so book the call the moment that you are ready.

The reason I want you to set up a call is so I can answer any questions that you have and to show you that getting your book done is excuse proof. Whether you write or speak out the book, the main thing is that there is no excuse not to have a completed draft done within the next 60-90 days.

I am also going to do something I have never offered in my books. If you use the link below and set up a call, I will make a limited time offer of 20% off our services including the Book Publishing Implementation Program, One-On-One VIP Coaching, Done For You Book Publishing Service, and Done For You Book Launch Marketing Service.

Typically, I only offer this special discount to members of the chamber of commerce and to fellow Rotarians. I do this to give back to my community. As you are spending time reading this book, I also consider you part of our community. If you are ready to grow your business and change your life for the better, I invite you to set up a call with me. Due to time constraints, the call must be limited to 15 minutes.

Are you ready to get started?

To set up your complementary strategy session with Paul go to www.GetPublishedSystem.com and click on the strategy session tab.

Chapter 19 Summary: Get Published

"The best time to plant a tree was 20 years ago. The second best time is now." Chinese Proverb

We have covered a lot of information in this book. By the time you have made it to this chapter (unless you skipped ahead to read the summary) you have read over twenty thousand words. This is the longest book I have written and the scary part is that we have only scratched the surface of book publishing.

There are many moving parts when it comes to writing, publishing, and launching your book, especially if you want your book to become a #1 bestseller. One question I get often is what exactly is a #1 bestseller?

Having a #1 bestseller is when your book is number one in at least one book category for a minimum of one week. Technically, most people will say that it doesn't matter if your book is a bestseller for an hour or six months, the moment you see that your book is number one in its category, then your book is a bestseller. In my view, and in my own bestseller guarantee, I define a bestseller as a book that is #1 in at least one category for a minimum of one week. The longer your book is a bestseller the better, as it will increase exposure and revenue for your book and your business.

The point is that your book peaked as a bestseller on Amazon and thus you are officially a bestselling author. It is harder than it seems, but by reading this book, joining our Get Published Facebook Community, and watching your complementary Get Published Webclass you will be in a much better position to succeed if you want to learn the process.

If you would like my team to publish your book for you, then I invite you to set up a quick call with me so we can talk about your book, as well as what you want to get out of it. Many business owners I have worked with do not have the time to learn about how to publish themselves and is why I have set up both our Done For You Book Publishing Service and our Done For You Book Launch Marketing Service.

Throughout the book, we have covered why everyone has a book within themselves, how to run your book like a business, choosing your book title and subtitle, designing your book cover, and outlining and either writing or speaking out your book. Creating your first draft through either writing your book or speaking out your book via the Rev app makes creating your book excuse proof as you can speak out your book throughout the day wherever you are.

Once your draft is completed, we covered the editing process, how to get your book formatted, creating a book description that sells, and how to get reviews.

We covered a brief overview of both the free and 99 cent book launch strategy, how to create your audiobook, how to build your audience, back-end offers, and revenue streams.

One thing I want to make clear is that no one can do it entirely themselves. We all need help! I am a huge believer in having help and I hired a business coach last year to help me. Hiring my coach and going through his program was the best decision I ever made. The money I invested in the program was significant, but you do get what you pay for. It was life changing when I decided to hire a coach to help me implement the framework for our Book Publishing Implementation Program.

Best part is that the investment often is tax deductible when you hire a coach and use a publisher to get published. Check with your countries tax laws, but I was able to write off the investment of hiring my own coach on my taxes. Coaching and publishing costs are often tax deductible and I want to mention that again as not everyone realizes the tax benefits in getting published. It is also great for writing travel books, as I was able to write off a significant amount of money from trips to Maui and San Diego as I wrote guidebooks while on vacation.

Having a book publishing coach brings focus, accountability, implementation, and support to getting your book created, published and marketed. It also will help build your business quickly with a proven system that works. The hardest part about publishing and marketing your book is the implementation process, which is the primary benefit you will get should we end up working together.

One of the most important questions that you need to ask yourself is this.

What are you willing to invest to change your life?

If you are reading this book then you are most likely at a fork in the road. You want to make a change.

QUESTION: WOULD YOU RATHER PUBLISH THE SAME WAY OR FOLLOW MY BOOK PUBLISHING SYSTEM AND WORK WITH ME?

The change you want to make involves either growing your business or starting a new business. If you are a business owner, having a book is essential to growing your business.

I was in that same situation three years ago when I wrote, published, and marketed my first book. At that time, I was making good money teaching, but I was not making a lot of additional income. After that trip to Las Vegas, I started to write my first book. Once the book was written, I realized that I needed more money to be able to pay for my first launch while waiting for the royalties to come in. Once your book is launched, it takes two months to get your first royalty check from Amazon.

I knew that I would be spending at least a couple thousand dollars with publishing and marketing my first book. Once I realized the investment that was necessary, I made the decision to ask my dad for a loan. I told him my business plan and he lent me two thousand dollars so I could get the book published and marketed properly.

That loan resulted in starting a business that now makes significant revenue three years later with multiple revenue streams on the front-end with each of my books in Kindle, audiobook, and paperback and on the back-end with speaking events, our Book Publishing Implementation Program, One-On-One VIP Coaching, Done For You Book Publishing and Done For You Book Launch Marketing Services.

Taking that risk three years ago enabled me to leave my job as a teacher, be my own boss, and set my own hours. The commute is now ten seconds from the living room to my home office and I love it. The best part is working with others to help them write, publish and market their books to a #1 bestseller and more importantly helping them change their lives.

Every one of my clients has become a #1 bestselling author and I take a lot of pride in that. We offer a proven system that will get you the outcome that you are looking for with becoming a #1 bestselling author and growing your business. I strongly recommend investing your time by reading this book, joining our Get Published

Facebook Community, and watching your complementary Get Published Webclass.

I would love to work with you either through having you join our Book Publishing Implementation Program, One-On-One VIP Coaching, Done For You Book Publishing and Done For You Book Launch Marketing Services.

Now it is time for you to decide and answer the following question one more time.

What are you willing to invest to change your life?

Please spread the word about our services if you know of others who are looking to get published. I also ask that you please pass this book on to your friends and family so they can also benefit from the information. If there is anything I can do for you then please let me know.

On the next page, you have an invitation to set up a strategy session with me. The call is NOT a sales presentation and my intention with the call is only to answer any questions that you have about the writing, publishing, and marketing process with your book.

Thank you for investing your time in reading my book. I look forward to speaking with you and helping in your author journey to get published.

To find out more about our services go to www.GetPublishedSystem.com and click on the services tab.

Strategy Session Invitation

Are you ready to set up a complimentary strategy session with Paul?

Are you ready to talk with Paul and learn how to get published with a proven system that works?

The call is NOT a sales presentation and Paul's intention with the call is only to answer any questions that you have about the writing, publishing, and marketing process with your book.

Due to time constraints, the call must be limited to 15-minutes.

Are you ready to get started?

To set up your complimentary strategy session go to our website at www.GetPublishedSystem.com and click on the strategy session tab.

More Books by Paul

"Quick and inexpensive reads for self-improvement, a healthier lifestyle, and book publishing"

Thirteen-time Amazon bestselling author, Paul Brodie believes that books should be inexpensive, straightforward, direct, and not have a bunch of fluff.

Each of his books were created to solve problems including living a healthy lifestyle, increasing motivation, improving positive thinking, traveling to amazing destinations, and helping authors write, publish and market their books to a #1 bestseller.

What makes Paul's books different is his ability to explain complex ideas and strategies in a simple, accessible way that you can implement immediately.

Go to www.GetPublishedSystem.com and click on the books tab to check out Paul's books.

About the Author

Paul Brodie the CEO of Brodie Consulting Group, which specializes in book publishing and coaching clients on how to write, publish, and market their books. He is also the President of BrodieEDU, an education consulting firm that specializes in giving motivational, business, publishing, and leadership seminars for universities and corporations.

Brodie left teaching in June 2017 after serving as an educator in multiple roles since 2008. He served as a Special Education Teacher from 2014-2017 in the Hurst-Euless-Bedford ISD (2014-2016) and Fort Worth ISD (2016-2017) while working specifically with special needs children who had Autism. In 2014-2015 he also served as the head tennis coach and lead the school to a district championship and an undefeated season.

From 2011-2014, Brodie served as a Grant Coordinator for the ASPIRE program in the Birdville Independent School District. As coordinator, he created instructional and enrichment programming for over 800 students and 100 parents in the ASPIRE before and after school programs. He also served on the Board of Directors for the Leadership Development Council, Inc. from 2005-2014 with leading the implementation of educational programming in low cost housing.

From 2008-2011, he was a highly successful teacher in Arlington, TX where he taught English as a Second Language. Brodie turned a once struggling ESL program into one of the top programs in the school district. Many of his students moved on to journalism, AVID, art classes, and many students exited the ESL program entirely.

Teaching methods during his career as an educator included daily writing practice, flash cards, picture cards, academic relays, music, movies, and short educational videos including the alphabet and sight words. Additional strategies included graphic novels paired with movie versions of the novels, games, cultural celebrations, and getting parents involved in their children's education. Brodie's approach has been called unconventional but very effective, revolutionary, and highly engaging. His students have always shown great improvement with both academics and behavior throughout the school year and he was honored to teach such an amazing and diverse group of students during his career as an educator.

Previously, Brodie spent many years in the corporate world and decided to leave a lucrative career in the medical field to follow his passion and transitioned into education. Prior to working in the medical field, he worked for Enterprise Rent-A-Car after receiving his Bachelor's Degree and for Savitz Research during his high school and college years. He is very grateful for every career opportunity as each one was an avenue to learn and grow.

Brodie earned an M.A. in Teaching from Louisiana College and B.B.A. in Management from the University of Texas at Arlington. Brodie is a bestselling author and has written multiple books. He wrote his first book, Eat Less and Move More: My Journey in the summer of 2015. Brodie's goal of the book was to help those like himself who had challenges with weight. The goal of his first book was to promote not only weight loss but also health and wellness. He is also the author of Motivation 101, Positivity Attracts, Book Publishing for Beginners, The Pursuit of Happiness, Maui (two Maui books), Just Do It, PMA, San Diego, Book Publishing for Authors, and Champion. All twelve books (available in Kindle, Paperback, and Audiobook) are Amazon bestsellers and are based on his motivational seminars, book publishing, love of travel, and struggles with weight.

His seminars have been featured at many universities and at leadership conferences across the United States since 2005. Brodie is active in professional organizations and within the community and currently serves on the Advisory Board for Advent Urban Youth Development and as a volunteer with the Special Olympics. Paul is a proud Rotarian and is a member of the Arlington Chamber of Commerce and the Arlington Chamber Young Professionals. He continues to be involved with The International Business Fraternity of Delta Sigma Pi and has served in many positions since 2002 including National Vice President – Organizational Development, Leadership Foundation Trustee, National Organizational Development Chair, District Director, and in many other volunteer leadership roles. He resides in Arlington, TX.

Acknowledgments

Thank you to God for guidance and protection throughout my life.

Thank YOU, the reader, for investing your time reading this book.

Thank you to my amazing mom, Barbara Brodie for all the years of support and a kick in the butt when needed.

Thank you to Billy Atwell and Sandra Joines for both writing great forewords for this book.

Thank you to my awesome sister, Dr. Heather Ottaway for all the help and feedback with my books and with my motivational seminars. It is scary how similar we are.

Thank you to Devin Mooneyham for serving as the editor of my book. The slicing and dicing as always was very much appreciated and I could not have gotten this book published without her assistance.

Thank you to all who have served on the BrodieEDU Advisory Board.

Thank you to my dad, Bill "The Wild Scotsman" Brodie for his encouragement and support with the business aspects of BrodieEDU and Brodie Consulting Group.

Thank you to Shannon and Robert Winckel (two members of the four horsemen with myself and our good friend, Derrada Rubell-Asbell) for their friendship and support. Shannon and Robert are two of my best teacher friends and are always great sounding boards for ideas.

Thank you to all the amazing friends that I have worked with over the past twenty plus years. Each of them has made a great impact on my life.

Thank you to all my students that I have had the honor to teach over the years. I am very proud of each of my kids.

Thank you to Delta Sigma Pi Business Fraternity. I learned a great deal about public speaking and leadership through the organization and every experience that I have had helped me become the person that I am today.

Thank you to my three best friends: J. Dean Craig, Jen Mamber, and Aaron Krzycki. We have gone through a lot together and I look forward to many more years of friendship.

Thank you to all the students past and present at the UT Arlington and UT Austin chapters of DSP. Both schools mean a lot to me and I look forward to seeing them again at some point soon.

Thank you to the Lott Family (Stacy, Kerry, Lexi, and Austin) for their friendship over the past eight years.

Thank you to Robin Clites for always taking care of things at the house with ensuring that Mom and I can always get that family vacation every year.

Contact Information

Go to our website at www.BrodieConsultingGroup.com and click on the speaking and keynotes tab to see why you should consider bringing Paul to your campus or organization.

Paul can be reached at Brodie@BrodieConsultingGroup.com

Website www.GetPublishedSystem.com

Publishing and Coaching Services www.GetPublishedSystem.com

Get Published Podcast www.GetPublishedPodcast.com

Join our Get Published Facebook Group

Follow Paul on Instagram

Follow Paul on Twitter @Get__Published

Like Paul's Author Page on Facebook

Feedback Request

Please leave a review for my book as I would greatly appreciate your feedback.

If for some reason you did not enjoy the book then please contact me via email at Brodie@BrodieConsultingGroup.com to discuss options prior to leaving a negative review and please feel free to let me know how the book can be improved.